THE SCIENCE COOKBOOK

Experiment-recipes that teach science and nutrition

Julia B. Waxter

Fearon Teacher Aids
Carthage, Illinois

Simon & Schuster Supplementary Education Group

Dedication

To Eleanor P. Graham, my science teacher

Acknowledgments

I would like to express appreciation for the advice of Dr. Paul R. Daniels, Professor of Education at the Johns Hopkins University; for the interest of Dr. Michael Bender, Director of Special Education at the John F. Kennedy Institute/Johns Hopkins School of Medicine; and for the inspiration of Dr. Nancy McK. Smith, my former principal at the Kennedy Institute Learning Disability School. I am also very grateful to Rudite Emir, editor, and to Gail Larrick and Peter R. Cross of Fearon Pitman Publishers (now Pitman Learning, Inc.) for their encouragement, care, and skillful editing.

Editors: Rudite Emir, Gail Larrick, and Peter Cross
Production editor: Zanae Jelletich
Designer: Rick Chafian
Illustrator: Rick Hackney
Cover designer: Mary Ann Schildknecht

ISBN–0–8224–6292–3
Library of Congress Catalog Card Number: 79–57431
Printed in the United States of America.
1.9 8

Preface

Observers in the Learning Disability School in the Kennedy Institute kitchen science classes are always intrigued by the intense involvement and high interest of the supposedly learning handicapped students. This program originated four years ago when we asked Julia Waxter to develop a cooking course for our disabled learners, about 90 percent of whom are boys. It quickly became one of the most popular courses in the curriculum, although unlike most cooking classes, relatively little eating goes on in it. Vocabulary development, scientific observation, math concepts, and fine motor development are some of the major objectives of the course.

In May 1977, samples of Mrs. Waxter's lessons and a videotape of one of her classes were presented at the International Reading Association meeting in Miami. Almost immediately, requests for more of her lessons were received at the institute. Teachers throughout the country, it seemed, wanted to try this highly motivating vehicle for both regular and mainstreamed special students. I encouraged Mrs. Waxter to compile her lessons, and am now pleased to see this book of them published.

Lest readers envision Mrs. Waxter as merely a scientific cook, let me add that she also teaches reading, social studies, and regular science classes. Her photography has been exhibited in local galleries, and she is also a hiker, popular hostess, and mother who holds degrees from Sweet Briar and the Johns Hopkins University.

Nancy McK. Smith
Former Principal,
John F. Kennedy Institute for
Handicapped Children

Contents

Introduction

The Science Cookbook presents experiments that are enjoyable simply as experiences, yet the book also presents a solid, structured course. It is not designed as a rigorous or theoretical science curriculum; rather, it is designed to encourage the curiosity of elementary and middle school students and to foster the development of these students' powers of observation.

This book gives teachers a practical and useful base from which to launch science, math, and language arts instruction. Parents who wish to make their children's learning experiences enjoyable and meaningful will find The Science Cookbook a valuable resource for introducing concepts of science and nutrition through cooking. The Science Cookbook can be used by scout leaders and teachers' aides as a basic introduction to scientific principles. Pre-school teachers can encourage participation, observation, and language development as they conduct the experiments. The lessons can also be adapted for use in teaching the learning disabled or the mentally retarded.

I developed the units for a kitchen science curriculum in the Learning Disability School in the Kennedy Institute for Handicapped Children. Most of the lessons were conducted during a one hour activities period, while extra time was needed for three experiments (see "Drying Apples," "Cooking Dried Lima Beans," and "Making Meringue Shells"). Five or six students attended this activity on a rotating basis once every two weeks. The classroom I used had a stove and kitchen equipment, but I also held classes in a regular classroom using a hotplate, since most of the experiments do not require the use of an oven.

In the classroom, one teacher can teach and supervise a classroom of students, scheduling an experiment from The Science Cookbook once a week. The experiments may be conducted as demonstrations with student participation, or the students may be divided into small groups to perform the experiments independently.

Using The Science Cookbook

The nine major scientific topics developed in The Science Cookbook encompass most of what takes place in an area of immediate concern to everyone: the preparation of food. As such, these topics provide a meaningful foundation for the conventional study of science.

In using the experiment-recipes and accompanying material, students will develop awarenesses in the areas of chemistry, physics, and biology. They will set up conditions for, and observe effects of, dissolving, oxidizing, and evaporating. They will discover how cooking procedures cause changes in food substances that create the familiar consistencies of many foods. For example, they will learn how heat coagulates protein, softens cellulose, and causes starch to thicken liquids. Awareness of scientific principles will expand as students separate oil particles or protein strands by mechanical means in order to change the physical nature of food substances. They will learn that, by physical or chemical processes, gas can be incorporated into a mixture and then expanded by heat to provide a leavening effect. And, finally, they will become more knowledgeable about their own physical senses as they add herbs and spices to various dishes.

The nine major topics explored in The Science Cookbook are apparent in the unit titles. Accompanying each title is a focus question which is answered via the experiments in that unit.

The introduction to each unit touches on a few areas applicable to the focus question. This introductory discussion will help the teacher, leader, or parent to refresh his or her knowledge of the subject and to anticipate questions that students may raise.

Inevitably, the subject matter in the units is interrelated. To foster this relationship, cross-references are interspersed parenthetically. Each one serves as a quick reminder of an opportunity to preview or review a principle or concept developed in another unit.

Following the introduction, the specific teaching goals of a unit are listed as the *Objectives*. Next, a list of *Applied Skills* suggests how students may gain from the experiments in such ways as measuring ingredients, developing motor dexterity, or using mathematical formulas.

A list of *Key Ideas* gives the basic understandings that are introduced in the experiments to answer the focus question. This section also lists related concepts which will develop as the lessons evolve.

Each experiment within a unit has its own brief introduction, providing information and instructions that I have found useful in teaching the lessons. In parentheses, I quote an occasional question or comment that I have used to guide the students to a particular discovery. Vocabulary words to be introduced and defined in the course of the experiments are italicized when first used in this introductory section in order to call your attention to them as you plan your discussions.

The *Vocabulary* list immediately follows the experiment introduction. It provides definitions for words related to the scientific concepts developed as well as for words useful in understanding the recipe. The asterisked vocabulary words are words that appear on the student experiment pages but not in your introductory material. These words are asterisked to draw attention to the fact that you will need to explain them even though they are not referred to in the introductory text.

Introduce the vocabulary before or during the activity. Make vocabulary cards or use a chalkboard for recording the words to provide visual reinforcement. Since the best opportunity for practicing new vocabulary will be during informal discussions with the students, be sure to make maximum use of the new words and call for their use throughout the activity.

A list of *Materials* gives you a quick check of what you will need for a given experiment. A hot plate will suffice as heat source, except for the few experiments in which an oven is specified. Most of the equipment called for is available in any kitchen. Certain basic items are *not* listed under Materials—a clock, pot holders, water, a vegetable

scrubbing brush, paper towels, and cleaning implements. These should be regularly available for the experiments.

The eating utensils specified are sufficient for six persons, the optimum size for a working unit. Such a group is small enough to sit around a table so that members can help one another. They can participate frequently and observe together by the stove. And, it is large enough to encourage brainstorming and learning to wait for a turn.

A few special pieces of equipment are suggested as optional: a steaming rack, or steaming basket, that adjusts to fit most pots (for several vegetable recipes), a food mill, and a pastry bag (for making Twice-Baked Potatoes). These implements are fun to manipulate as well as effective. A small scale also adds an element of interest and an opportunity to teach math each time an ingredient is called for in weighed ounces.

Discussion Questions are provided for an informal review of each experiment with the students and as a means of evaluation. Those using the experiments as science lessons in schools will want to keep these questions in mind as they proceed through the experiment.

A list of *Related Activities* suggests additional experiments and projects to further apply and reinforce the scientific principles covered in a unit. This section may suggest library research, field trips, alternative recipes, or other activities for expanding selected concepts developed in a given experiment.

The actual *Experiments* can be found on pages 55–82. These student worksheets are intended for the students' direct use. Permission is granted to copy this page, so that each child in a group can have his or her own sheet for easy reference. Copies can be laminated to cards to make them more durable.

Each experiment is usually, but not always, a recipe. The recipes will serve small tasting portions to six people. These portions are too small to spoil one's appetite before lunch or to appear unappetizing after lunch. To allow for different quantities and to provide practice in computation, some recipes call for cutting the recipe in half or for multiplying the quantities by several factors.

Goals

In formulating the directions on the experiment pages as well as in providing suggestions for discussions, I have kept several points in mind:

1. Experimenting and cooking by following written directions motivate reading. You will want to foster language skills guided by the individual needs of the students. It will seem natural to encourage some of the following cognitive, reading, and expressive skills while the experiments are being discussed and carried out:

- listening
- following oral directions
- applying word-attack techniques
- recognizing words and distinguishing between them
- labeling and recording
- following written directions
- answering comprehension questions

2. Learning fundamental scientific concepts and using the scientific method are basic goals. The scientific techniques that can be practiced during the experiments include:

- hypothesizing ("What will happen if . . . ?")
- labeling
- measuring accurately
- observing
- collecting data
- comparing
- categorizing
- drawing conclusions
- summarizing

3. Developing motor skills with kitchen tools and applying math skills complement the above goals by providing students with additional opportunities to enhance their self-esteem.

Motivation

With the listed skills and concepts as the ultimate goals, the obvious motivation for each experiment will be the finished product. Four other elements also basic to the cooking experiences will provide motivation:

1. *Healthful and appealing ingredients.* Crisp vegetables, toasted wheat germ, golden honey, and other nutritious ingredients are attractive and appetizing.

2. *Hands-on involvement.* The student who reads one item of a recipe should be the one to locate and measure the specific ingredient. Another student may read ahead in order to carry out one of the directions. Sharing a common goal, other members of the group will be motivated to lend a helping hand.

If one of the goals is to teach word recognition, allow students to scan bags from health food stores or containers you have labeled yourself rather than the familiar commercial packages. Novel containers are suggestive of an exciting treasure hunt and create an exciting atmosphere.

3. *Hypothesizing about "What will happen if . . . ?"* Ask such questions to intrigue and encourage learning by observation. Be ready to supply some answers, though, so that the students are not straining to hypothesize too extensively for too long—this creates frustration.

4. *A hands-off attitude.* Allow plenty of time for students to do their own work. Gently call for checking if "teaspoon" is read as "tablespoon," "sugar" as "salt," or "cloves" as "chives." Encourage involvement. Let students solve their own problems, make errors, and try again. Let them discover ways to pour, beat, and measure. They will develop confidence from their many successes.

You may feel frustration as the students move slowly through tasks you could do far more quickly. They may pour a tablespoon of oil with exasperating deliberateness. They may be awkward in cutting the eyes out of potatoes, and they may ask why potatoes have eyes in the first place. It is worth "winding down" your own tempo and relaxing so that you can watch *them* enjoying the task in their own way. One student may demonstrate real skill in chopping vegetables with finesse. Another may show a new social awareness by spontaneously holding a bowl while a partner beats the ingredients. Thus, you may have a much-needed opportunity to give genuine praise for a specific behavior, something all of us need and like.

Teaching Approach

As the students are about to begin an experiment, stress the importance of following the directions in the order given. The experiment may be read through once, then discussed, and read again, one step at a time, or the directions may be simply read and followed step by step. Either way, make sure everyone is sure that step 1 has been completed before they tackle step 2.

Noses must not be so deep in the directions, however, that the students fail to notice what is happening. They should have time to express their observations, use new vocabulary, and formulate concepts.

Math concepts as well as science concepts can be reinforced as the activity proceeds. Seize opportunities for applying skills already learned, for clarifying uncertainties, and for previewing future concepts. The recipes offer the perfect opportunity to apply and manipulate fractions using measuring cups and spoons.

Encourage the students to help explain the abstract concepts to each other. I once used Cuisenaire rods to illustrate ½ of 1½ and then expanded the demonstration by using diagrams of pies and measuring cups of water. But a student clinched the idea in this particular group by explaining to the others that 1½ dollars is equal to 6 quarters, and half of that is 3 quarters (¾).

Some Practical Tips

These suggestions may be helpful in developing skills:

- Post two 5 × 7 inch cards, one under the other, with *teaspoon* written on one and *tablespoon* on the other. Supply measuring spoons which have the corresponding words clearly marked. Encourage everyone to double check teaspoon and tablespoon when reading the list of ingredients and selecting the correct measuring spoon.

- Supply cup, pint, and quart measures. Compare how 1 cup of water registers in each container. Relate this to ½ pint and ¼ quart.

- Include time as a measurement. Use a clock rather than a timer in order to develop facility in adding minutes to any given time.

At the start, clarify some basic safety rules to be observed throughout the experiments:

- Be aware of stove settings.

- Keep pan handles away from the stove's edge.
- Use potholders.
- Set aside breakable items and containers of ingredients when not in use.

Also review health rules:

- Wash hands before preparing foods. (But cool the sanitary ardor of those finicky students who want to wash every minute.)
- Keep hands away from mouth and hair and from dirty surfaces.
- Cover sneezes and coughs. Wash hands again before handling food.
- Scrub fruits and vegetables to remove chemicals and dirt. Use cold water.

Try these solutions to avoid the mess that can accompany cooking:

- Self-appointed cleaners often straighten or wipe up as the activity proceeds. Gently encourage this.
- Job appointments can be made by means of a chart, or more informally. Rotate jobs for each experiment. (Use paper towels to dry dishes, as a convenience and a health precaution.)

Extending and Improvising

As you try out the experiments, you may need to modify some of them to fit the capabilities of the students. Perhaps you will think of recipes of your own to write up for an appropriate unit. You may want to investigate why certain phenomena happen, or you may want to find additional information about certain foods. (See the BIBLIOGRAPHY, page 47, for ideas and inspiration.)

Your enthusiasm will be contagious. Your students will not only feel useful and gain confidence, but they will eagerly add to their store of concepts, thus enjoying both the tangible and intangible fruits of their labors.

1

Dissolution: How Does Temperature Affect Dissolving Rate?

In this unit, students investigate the effect of temperature on molecular activity, or the speed at which molecules move. Dissolving takes place when molecules separate from each other and spread out, or diffuse, into a solvent. Temperature is a spectacular factor in determining whether this action will happen in a few seconds or in many hours. Whether hot or cold, molecules of all matter are in constant motion. Applying heat gives molecules extra energy and steps up their activity; chilling reduces their energy and slows down their movement.

Despite their activity, molecules of the same kind have an attraction toward each other which is a force called cohesion. There is always a lot of space between molecules, but when they are cool, they are relatively close together. Then the cohesion is very strong, and the molecules assume a solid form. When they gain energy from heat, the molecules move apart. Then, the cohesion is weaker, and the molecules take on a liquid form. In a gas, cohesion is so weak and activity so great that the molecules travel far apart in all directions; the volume of a gas is limited only by the container it is put in.

When honey is mixed with water, the ever-moving molecules of honey bombard themselves into the spaces between the ever-moving molecules of water, and vice versa. There they are attracted to the water molecules, to some degree, by a force called adhesion, or attraction of one kind of molecule to another kind. We say that the honey is dissolved, or if we are being scientifically precise, that the molecules of the honey have diffused among the water molecules. The hotter the liquid, the faster the process occurs.

Some kinds of molecules do not separate (diffuse) into any liquid, and some molecules can diffuse into some liquids but not others (for example, grease into gasoline, but not into water). Dissolving some substances (for example, salt in water) involves the separation of the solute into ions rather than molecules, but this distinction is not developed in the following discussion.

Objectives

- To teach the concepts of molecular activity and molecular forces of cohesion and adhesion
- To relate the processes of dissolving and diffusion to the above concepts
- To demonstrate the effect of temperature on molecular activity
- To introduce hypothesizing, labeling, measurement, observation, and comparison within an experimental framework
- To encourage computation of required amounts for servings needed

Applied Skills

Motor Skills: squeezing lemons, pouring

Measuring: measuring volume and temperature

Estimating: estimating the amount of juice in a lemon

Computing: multiplying, subtracting

Observing: watching dissolving rate, noting diffusion of flavor

Key Ideas

- Every kind of matter is composed of molecules.
- Spaces exist between molecules of all matter.
- All molecules are in constant motion.
- Heat increases the activity of molecules.
- Molecules of the solute diffuse throughout the solvent.
- Temperature increases the dissolving rate of a solute.
- The freezing point of water is 32°F.; the boiling point is 212°F. at sea level.

Student worksheet, p. 55.

DISSOLUTION EXPERIMENT: MAKING A SOLUTION

When you *dissolve* honey, it seems to disappear but it doesn't go away; its *molecules* simply *diffuse* among the water molecules. ("Taste it. Has the honey gone away?") Hypothesize before the experiment as to which water temperature will be most effective in dissolving the honey. ("Who is betting on which temperature?") As the students prepare the three glasses of water, let them follow the changing thermometer readings. ("What is room temperature? At what temperature does water boil? At what temperature do you think it freezes?") Watch the honey disappear in the *liquid* and discuss what is happening to its molecules. Compare the tastes of the *solutions*.

Introduce the vocabulary using prepared cards or the chalkboard. Underline *sol* where it appears in the words, as in dis<u>sol</u>ve. Use the vocabulary throughout the experiment and in the

discussion, emphasizing *solvent* for the water and *solute* for the honey.

Vocabulary

diffuse to spread out in every direction

dissolve to mix a substance (solute) with a liquid (solvent) so that the molecules of the substance diffuse throughout the liquid

*ingredient a substance that is used in a mixture to combine with other substances in the same mixture

liquid a substance that flows freely and changes shape, such as water

molecules the smallest particles of any substance that retain the properties of that substance

solute the substance which is dissolved by the solvent

solution a mixture formed by dissolving a solute in a solvent

solvent a substance which dissolves another substance

Materials

3 clear glasses or glass jars

3 labels

measuring cups and spoons

pitcher

pan to heat water

thermometers to measure water at 32° F., room temperature, and boiling

stove or hot plate

teaspoon for each student

ingredients listed on the experiment page

Discussion Questions

- What was our solute?
- At what temperature did the solute dissolve the fastest?
- At what temperature did the solute diffuse the best?
- If you put sugar in water, which would be the solvent and which would be the solute?
- Where does the solute go when it can no longer be seen?
- Why does heat make the solute dissolve and diffuse quickly?

Related Activities

- Try dissolving other substances (flour, butter, sugar, dirt) in hot and cold water. Observe the effectiveness of water as a solvent of these various substances and compare the results.

- Add detergent to water and observe its effectiveness in dissolving oil. Try gasoline or a cleaning fluid (in very small quantities and with *great* care) as an oil solvent and compare its effectiveness with that of the detergent.

- Dissolve some honey in water. Boil off the water gently until the honey can be seen again, to prove that dissolving has not altered the basic nature of the honey.

- Discuss the effect of temperature on the metabolism of cold-blooded animals.

Student worksheet, p. 56.

DISSOLUTION EXPERIMENT: MAKING HONEY LEMONADE

Children will often ask, "Is this honey made by bees?" and you can assure them that it is; there is no such thing as human-made honey. As a worker bee visits flowers in spring and summer, it collects *pollen* on its legs and body while sucking up *nectar* with its tongue. Pollen and nectar are food for the young bees developing in the hive; nectar is also stored in wax compartments in the hive, and water is removed from it, thickening it into honey. The stored honey is the basic food (energy source) for the adult bees, and its storage allows the colony to survive through the winter, under most conditions. Usually there is more than enough for their needs.

People began to help themselves to bees' food and use it for sweetening long before they discovered that they could manufacture sugar from sugar cane and sugar beets. The sugar molecules in honey (glucose and fructose) are simpler molecular forms of sugar than those found in cane and beets (sucrose).

The ingredients for making honey lemonade are calculated so that the solutions saved from the Making a Solution experiment can be used. When more than three persons are to be served, the quantity of additional ingredients needed can be found by using the formula on the experiment page. The meaning of the parentheses in the formula may need to be explained. If the solutions from the previous experiment are not used, the students can multiply the amounts supplied for one person by the number of persons to be served.

Ask the students to estimate how many tablespoons of lemon juice can be squeezed from a particular lemon. After squeezing the lemon, let them measure the juice to see how close they came with their estimates.

Vocabulary

nectar the sweet liquid flowing from the nectary glands at the bottom of a flower blossom (Through its attraction of pollen-carrying insects, nectar ensures pollination, the process by which flowers get fertilized for production of seeds.)

pollen powder, often yellow, produced at the top of the stamen of a flower and acting as a fertilizing agent in the production of seeds

Materials

pitcher
measuring cups and spoons
reamer (juice extractor)
large spoon
paper cup or glass for each student
ingredients listed on experiment page

Discussion Questions

- Why shouldn't you use ice water when using honey to make lemonade?
- Why does the recipe call for ice?
- Why isn't it a good idea to use boiling water to make lemonade?
- How does stirring affect the dissolving rate of a substance?
- What would happen if you did not stir?
- Does lemon juice diffuse in water?
- Does honey dissolve in lemonade?
- How many teaspoons make one tablespoon?
- How many tablespoons make one cup?

Related Activities

- Use leftover honey lemonade to make soda pop. Add ½ teaspoon baking soda to each glass.

- Compare a solution to a suspension (a mixture in which a solid is diffused in a liquid without the solid being dissolved). Explain that the visible lemon particles in lemonade are suspended for a time after mixing, as are particles of flour or dirt in water. Later the larger particles will settle to the bottom.

- Use a globe or map to locate areas where lemons are grown.

- Collect information on lemons, limes, and other citrus fruits.

- Investigate the story of scurvy in the British navy, and the discovery of its cause by Dr. James Lind in 1747.

- Learn about the life of bees.

- Study the structure of a flower to understand the sources and functions of pollen and nectar.

2

Oxidation: How Does Oxygen in the Air Affect Foods?

Some changes in food are physical; when honey is dissolved in water, the honey molecules separate (see DISSOLUTION, page 5.) However, when molecules of oxygen from the air combine with certain substances in foods, the change is chemical, and oxidation takes place. Whereas a honey molecule remains a honey molecule even after it has dissolved, an oxidized molecule, having combined with oxygen, becomes a new material—an oxide.

Oxidation includes the chemical processes of burning and rusting, as well as the discoloring of fruits and vegetables. It also occurs in human metabolism to produce energy from food (see THICKENING, page 26). In this unit, the common meaning of oxidation is used, and oxygen is the only oxidizer considered.

Fast oxidation is called combustion. It can produce so much heat that light is produced, in the form of fire or even an explosion. In the human body, oxidation is slower, but it still causes heat, which keeps us warm and provides energy. Rusting and discoloration are such slow oxidation processes that one cannot readily measure the small amount of heat generated.

If you want to prevent oxidation of a material, keep oxygen away from it: smother a fire, paint iron, or coat fruits and vegetables with ascorbic acid (vitamin C). Ascorbic acid (and other antioxidants) combines with oxygen and creates a protective, colorless covering of oxidized material

(oxide). Oxygen gas, though readily available (comprising 21 percent of the gases in air), cannot easily penetrate the oxide to combine with the fruit. Without the ascorbic acid, oxygen combines with the fruit and creates an unappetizing, brown covering of oxidized material.

Objectives

- To develop the concept that oxidation is vital to life and is evident in a variety of processes
- To demonstrate the effects of oxidation on fruits and vegetables
- To establish the principle that oxidation can be slowed down

Applied Skills

Motor skills: squeezing lemons, cutting fruits, slicing potatoes with a peeler, coordinating movements in turning over a potato cake

Measuring: measuring volume

Computing: finding 1/3 of a group of objects

Observing: comparing discoloration of fruits and of potatoes

Key Ideas

- Oxidation occurs when oxygen combines with another substance.

9

- Rusting, burning, and human metabolism are forms of oxidation.
- Many fruits and vegetables contain substances which oxidize.
- Ascorbic acid protects fruits against oxidation.

Student worksheet, p. 57.

OXIDATION EXPERIMENT: WATCHING AIR DISCOLOR FRESH FRUIT

Whether we know it or not, almost every one of us has observed the *oxidation* of foods. ("What happens to an apple if you set it down for a while after you have bitten into it?") Apple skin not only keeps the apple from drying out (see EVAPORATION, page 12), but it also protects the fruit from contact with *oxygen*. Once the apple skin is broken, oxidation begins. Oxidation not only discolors the fruit, but also changes and destroys valuable vitamins and minerals.

This experiment will demonstrate that dipping fruit in vitamin C protects it from oxidation. For comparison, dip some apple slices in water. The water will simply evaporate, and the fruit will begin to oxidize. If you hold some apple slices under water, you will prevent oxygen from reaching the surface of the fruit, but you will also allow valuable nutrients to diffuse into the water.

If you put some cut fruit into the refrigerator, you will discover that oxidation will be slower there than at room temperature because molecular activity slows down with a decrease in temperature. Coating cut fruit with vitamin C (an *antioxidant*) and refrigerating it is the best method of *inhibiting* oxidation. The way to preserve the most nutrients is to cut the fruit at the last possible minute before serving it.

Although the fruit that has been oxidized does not look very appetizing, it is not spoiled. Use all the cut fruit to fill meringue shells (see Making Meringue Shells, page 32) and add a topping of whipped cream (see Making Whipped Cream, page 33) for a delicious dessert.

Vocabulary

antioxidant a material which keeps a substance from combining with oxygen

*control (noun) a standard of comparison by which to check the results of an experiment

inhibit to hold an action in check, or to slow it down considerably

oxidation the combining of oxygen with molecules of another substance to make a new substance; the process causing such changes as rusting of iron and discoloring of fruits

oxygen a colorless, tasteless, odorless gas making up about 21 percent of the gases in the air

Materials

3 flat dishes (not metal)

3 labels

measuring cup

reamer (juice extractor)

paring knives

peelers (optional)

2 small bowls (not metal)

cutting board

bowl and spoon for each student

ingredients listed on experiment page

Discussion Questions

- How does apple skin protect an apple?
- Why does fruit turn brown after it is cut?
- What substance inhibits oxidation?
- How do lemons and other citrus fruits inhibit oxidation?

Related Activities

- Put another dish of fruit in the refrigerator and observe the effect of temperature on oxidation (see DISSOLUTION, page 5).
- Learn how and where the fruits used in the experiment are grown.
- Compare and categorize the seed formations in the fruits used (core, stone, or berry seed). Citrus fruits are actually pulpy berries.
- Visit a produce market and categorize the fruits in families.

- Find exotic fruits, name them, and study their characteristics.
- Plant fruit seeds.

Student worksheet, p. 58.

OXIDATION EXPERIMENT: MAKING SLIM-SLICE POTATO CAKE

Warm temperatures speed oxidation, but what does the high heat of cooking do? ("Will an apple turn brown if you boil it? How about a potato?") Several cooking methods inhibit oxidation, because high heat renders *enzymes* inactive. When enzymes are present and active, they help oxygen combine with substances found in certain fruits and vegetables, which then turn brown.

When we boil a peeled potato, it will stay white, but not just because it is covered with water in the pot. When we rest a potato on a steaming rack above boiling water, it will remain as white as the boiled one. In both cases, heat inactivates the oxidizing enzymes. When we coat potato slices with oil and pan fry them, not only does the oil protect the potato from the air, but also the heat destroys the activity of the enzymes.

When very thin slices of potato are peeled off for this experiment, they will begin to oxidize immediately. Review the concept of oxidation (and how you can prevent it) by covering some slices with plastic, refrigerating some, and exposing some to air.

Thinly slicing potatoes is also the first step in making potato chips. Soak a few slices in water. They will look like potato chips when they absorb some liquid. Discuss the method of cooking them.

The frying process causes a crust to form on the potato cake ("How does the crust help prevent oxidation?"). Wait till the crust is thick enough to hold the cake together before attempting the tricky maneuver of turning over the whole mass. When you cut the cake, inspect the layer between the crusts to decide whether oxidation proceeded any further during the cooking process. ("What happens when you cut the cake? Will oxidation begin where the crust is not protecting the cake?").

Vocabulary

enzyme plant or animal substance which fosters reactions between chemicals without being changed itself

*eyes (potato) buds of a potato which can sprout to make potato plants

*skillet a frying pan

*wedge a shape that narrows from a wide end to a pointed tip, like the shape of a pie slice

Materials

medium skillet with lid

stove or hot plate

2 spatulas to turn potato cake

measuring spoons

peelers

paring knives

knife to cut potato cake

fork and plate for each student

ingredients listed on experiment page

Discussion Questions

- Why do certain foods turn brown when exposed to air?
- How does heat prevent oxidation?
- How does oil prevent oxidation?
- How does a crust prevent oxidation?

Related Activities

- Discuss the germination of potato eyes in comparison with that of seeds and grains (see Growing Wheat Sprouts, page 38).
- Soak a few thin slices of potato in water. Learn about the absorption of water by plant cells.
- Visit a potato chip factory.
- For other activities involving potatoes, see Making Twice-Baked Potatoes, Related Activities, page 25.

3

Evaporation and Absorption: How Do Removing and Restoring Water Affect Substances?

The earliest humans began to save their extra food by drying it in the sun or storing it in caves. They had learned that removing moisture from foods and keeping foods cool are two methods of slowing decay (see DISSOLUTION, page 5).

Several types of activity are taking place within fresh fruits and vegetables that contain a normal amount of water. Enzymes are catalysts, present in all living materials, that facilitate or speed chemical reactions. They are at work helping the ripening process of fruits and vegetables. The enzymes within an apple, for instance, continue to break down starches and turn them into sugar, even after the apple is picked. Thus you could say that the apple is "alive" when you bite into it. Of course, if you don't eat the apple, and enzyme activity is allowed to continue, overripening results. Enzymes also speed the oxidation of many foods, which turns them brown on the surface (see OXIDATION, page 9).

Another activity taking place in foods is caused by microorganisms—bacteria and molds from the air, the soil, and our entire environment. Little by little these organisms digest particles of food, thereby decomposing it. The waste from this digesting process is what we sometimes call decay. In many cases, this waste is poisonous, but it can also be beneficial. Carbon dioxide, for instance, is waste given off from living yeast that causes bread to rise (see LEAVENING, page 35). Another useful waste product is compost, decayed vegetable matter used to nourish plants.

The action of enzymes and microorganisms is inhibited by the absence of water. Therefore, to preserve food, we dry it by forcing water molecules to evaporate. When they evaporate, the molecules spread out into the air after the liquid has changed into a gas. Dried food will keep for months. Then if we soak it in water, it will absorb moisture and be restored to something similar to its original state.

Besides preserving foods, evaporation is also useful in cooking because it concentrates the essences and thickens the substance. Also, evaporation in a slow oven can restore the crunch to a soggy food by removing the moisture it has absorbed from the air. (One humid day, a little tot I knew bit into a cracker and complained, "Mommy, this cracker doesn't make any noise." A half hour in a 200° oven could have restored the cracker's noise potential.)

Objectives

- To impart an understanding of the processes of ripening and decaying and their dependence on moisture
- To explain the difference between the liquid and gaseous states of water
- To relate the concept of molecular activity to evaporation
- To teach a drying technique and relate it to preserving foods

12

Applied Skills

Motor skills: fanning, paring apples, slicing apples into rings, chopping vegetables

Hypothesizing: speculating as to how water can be evaporated quickly

Observing: observing boiling, watching the effects of evaporation and vaporization, comparing dehydrated and rehydrated beans, comparing fresh and dried fruit

Measuring: includes measurement of volume, weight, and diameter

Data collecting: tabulating times, weights, and sizes

Computing: adding mixed numbers, comparing speeds of evaporation, comparing sizes and weights of substances, averaging losses in size and weight

Key Ideas

- Evaporation is a change from a liquid state to a gaseous state.
- Both heat and air circulation speed up the process of evaporation.
- Fruits and vegetables contain large proportions of water.
- Moisture, combined with the activity of enzymes and microorganisms, promotes ripening and decay.
- Drying, or the evaporation of moisture, retards decay of foods.
- Water can be reabsorbed by dried substances.
- Taste, texture, size, and weight are affected by the amount of moisture taken from or added to a given food.

Student worksheet, p. 59.

EVAPORATION EXPERIMENT: EVAPORATING WATER

Water is found in one of three forms or *states:* the *solid* state (ice), the liquid state, and the *gaseous* state (*vapor*). These three forms are a result of the speed at which the molecules travel. The smallest particle of water is a molecule. Molecules are in constant motion. They may be restrained within a solid form (analogous to people in a football huddle), or a liquid form (analogous to people dancing closely and slowly), or they may move freely as a gas (analogous to people running around a playground).

While they are moving about in a liquid state, some molecules can move from the surface of the liquid into the surrounding air, that is, they can *evaporate.* ("How can you make water disappear without wiping it away?") The warmer the molecules are, the faster they move (see DISSOLUTION, page 5) and the more rapidly evaporation takes place.

Molecules move more easily into dry air than into moist air, which has many other water molecules already moving about. ("What will happen to a wet streak on a chalkboard if you fan it?") If the air above the water does not circulate, it becomes saturated with evaporated water molecules. Fanning away, or circulating, the water-saturated air will bring in some new, drier air. The water molecules will quickly evaporate into the drier air.

The quickest way to evaporate water is to boil it. At 212°F., and at lower temperatures above sea level, water turns into a vapor. ("What makes the bubbles form in boiling water?") The turbulence of boiling is caused by water molecules erupting in a gaseous form from the liquid. At 212°F., the molecules overcome their cohesive attraction (see DISSOLUTION, page 5) and can move easily into the air from the surface of the liquid.

Vocabulary

evaporate to pass from a liquid state into a gaseous state

gas a substance that has no shape or volume and will expand in all directions if uncontained

solid a substance, such as wood, which has a shape and cannot flow

state the condition or given form of a substance, such as the "liquid state"

vapor a gas; small particles diffused in the air, such as water suspended in air to form fog

Materials

2 metal pie pans

measuring spoons

stove or hot plate

chalkboard

sponge

a newspaper, cookie sheet, or fan

clock or stopwatch

pencils

copy of Table 1 for each student

Discussion Questions

• What conditions speed up evaporation?

• What can you see happening in and around the pan when water boils?

• Why should circulating air, by fanning, speed up evaporation?

• What helps wet clothes and dishes to dry?

• How does air above a lake compare with air in a desert?

Related Activities

• Try the evaporation experiment with 1 table-spoon of water in a closed and an open jar placed in a sunny window.

• Develop the concept of condensation, which is conversion from a gaseous to a liquid state, the opposite of evaporation.

• Study the hydrologic cycle: evaporation, cloud formation, and precipitation.

• Record and compare conditions on humid and dry days and the rates of evaporation on those days.

• Record and compare the temperature and rate of evaporation on hot and cold days.

Student worksheet, p. 60.

EVAPORATION EXPERIMENT: MAKING STEWED TOMATOES

When is a vegetable a fruit? A tomato is the fruit of the tomato plant. It is classified as a berry because of its many seeds and its pulpy texture. The Indians had already cultivated the tomato when the Spanish explorers came to South America. Seeds were taken back to Europe, and the new fruit came to be known as the "love apple." Considered poisonous by most people, it was used as an ornament in flower gardens. Only in the last hundred years have tomatoes become accepted as food in the United States.

The fruits of plants related to the tomato plant seem to be a diverse lot, but if you study the seeds of tomatoes, green peppers, and eggplants, you will realize how similar they are. When the seeds germinate, you can hardly distinguish the tiny plants from one another.

A tomato is almost all water. When you boil tomatoes, much of their water evaporates, leaving the *essence* of the tomato. ("How full is the pan compared with when we first put in the tomatoes?") The process *concentrates* the flavor and thickens the consistency.

The vapor or mist above the stewing tomatoes is made up of tiny droplets of water, which *condense* from the evaporated, gaseous state. The water first evaporates in the pan, then condenses above the pan, and then evaporates again in the air beyond the stove. If the gaseous water strikes a cold window pane, it will again condense, turning to water droplets on the window.

Tomato catsup is made from the essence of tomatoes. ("How do you think it's made?") To make catsup, tomatoes are cooked with ingredients similar to those used in making stewed tomatoes, plus other spices and vinegar. The seeds are strained out, and at least half of the water from the tomatoes is evaporated by cooking. Spaghetti sauce is *simmered* down, or else thickened with tomato paste. Tomato paste is made from tomatoes *dehydrated* by hours of cooking; the mass is then strained and placed in ovens or in the sun to thicken further.

Vocabulary

concentrate (verb) to make less dilute, more dense (or stronger and less watery)

condense to change from a gas to a liquid

dehydrate to remove water from a substance, to dry out

essence the fundamental part of something, the most important part of something

*optional suggested, but not necessary

simmer to cook slowly, just below boiling temperature

Materials

can opener

knife with broad, dull blade

serrated knives

cutting board

measuring spoons

mixing spoon

large frying pan with lid

stove or hot plate

fork and plate for each student

ingredients listed on experiment page

Discussion Questions

- What do you see in the air above the pan as the tomatoes cook?

- When does moisture appear on the inside of a kitchen window?

- What flavors can you taste in the stewed tomatoes?

- What has to be done to fresh tomatoes before they can be used for making pizza?

- What happens to the flavor of tomatoes when most of the water has evaporated?

- What is concentrated orange juice? Why do you add water to it?

Related Activities

- Make fried apples: Add water to sliced apples in a frying pan; cover them and cook until soft (about 10–15 minutes); then cook them uncovered to evaporate excess water (add butter, brown sugar, and cinnamon at this last stage).

- Find out how orange juice is dehydrated under low pressure before it is frozen.

- Grow tomatoes, peppers, and eggplants from seed.

- Make tomato catsup.

- Learn about the history of garlic and how it grows.

Student worksheet, p. 61.

EVAPORATION EXPERIMENT: DRYING APPLES

Indians used the sun for evaporating *moisture* from fruits and vegetables to *preserve* them. ("How are raisins made? Will they spoil as easily as grapes?") Now there are many refinements in the process of drying foods, including the use of ovens, antioxidants (see OXIDATION, page 9), steam blanching, sulfuring, and pasteurizing. Tests have been developed to make sure that foods have been dried enough to inhibit all *bacteria*, *molds*, and enzymes. Today, sun drying is recommended only in clean, low-humidity areas.

The apple drying experiment given here is almost as basic as the Indian method. To completely imitate the primitive method of preserving apples, dry them on three consecutive, hot, clear days, bringing the fruit in each night. However, an oven with a thermometer is recommended as a simpler, more predictable way of observing the effects of drying.

An antioxidant is optional, yet the use of lemon juice is an effective and inexpensive way of reinforcing the concept of oxidation. Vitamin C tablets are also adequate, although the binders and fillers in them cause cloudiness in the solution. Pure *ascorbic acid* is more expensive; it can be obtained at a pharmacy or in a prepared mixture at food markets, in the canning supplies department.

Have a Red Delicious apple available to compare with a Winesap, Jonathan, or York apple for tartness. ("Which apples have the most flavor?") The flavor of a dried apple is very important, because when an apple loses its water, it loses its pleasant crunchy texture.

To keep the apple rings away from the corroding and uneven heating effects of metal, make a temporary wooden drying rack by gluing the ends of dowels to slats, or put eight to ten layers of paper towels over a thin piece of plywood about 12 inches square. Make sure the drying rack will fit easily into the oven or dehydrator.

The weight loss is spectacular when apples are dried, dramatically illustrating the high water content of apples. Although greatly *shriveled*, dried apples make a tasty and nutritious snack.

Vocabulary

ascorbic acid vitamin C, found in many fresh foods, especially citrus fruits such as oranges and lemons

bacteria microscopic forms of life which help in digestion, ripening, and fermentation, and also cause disease, poisoning, and decay

moisture a small amount of liquid which is diffused; wetness; dampness

mold a wooly, fungus growth—actually simple plants—produced on damp or decaying material from other plants and animals

preserve to prepare a substance so as to protect it from decaying

shrivel to wrinkle and become smaller, often from drying

Materials

oven or food dryer/dehydrator

oven thermometer to indicate 150°F.

peelers

apple corer

serrated knives

cutting board

reamer (juice extractor)

scales to measure ounces

pie pan in which to weigh apples

shallow glass bowl for antioxidant

measuring spoons if vitamin C pills are used

wooden rack, approximately 12 inches square, or thin plywood board and 20 paper towels

ingredients listed on experiment page

pencils

copy of Table 2 for each student

Discussion Questions

• Why does drying apples keep the apples from decaying?

• Why is it helpful to turn the apples frequently as they dry?

• What would happen if you tried to dry the apples at a high temperature?

• Why is an apple ring smaller after it is dried?

• How much of the original apples seems to have been water?

• How much of the original apples seems to have been solid matter?

• How does concentrating the essence of an apple affect its flavor?

Related Activities

• Dry different kinds of apples. Decide which you like best.

• Experiment with fruits that have been left in open and closed jars in a warm place. Observe the development of decay. Examine molds with a magnifying glass.

• Read about the eating habits of Indians and early settlers and find out what other foods they dried to preserve them.

• Study various methods of food preservation: smoking, freezing, canning, cold storage, and the adding of chemical preservatives.

• Restore soggy crackers or cookies to crispness in a slow oven (200°F.).

Student worksheet, p. 62.

ABSORPTION EXPERIMENT: COOKING DRIED LIMA BEANS

Maybe the beans that Jack's mother threw out the window in the story "Jack and the Beanstalk" were lima beans, for their stalks can grow very tall. After the plants bloom, a pod develops; the seeds inside the pod are the beans. When allowed to overripen, the pods and seeds dry and shrivel right on the vine. Most of a bean's substance is potential nourishment for the tiny *embryo* inside, nourishment to be used when the bean is planted, to foster the growth of roots, stalk, and leaves.

Like tomatoes, lima beans were developed by Indians in South America and later adopted by explorers. They dry out so thoroughly that they can keep for years, but they are so hard when dry that before they can be eaten, they must be soaked and cooked for a long time or else sprouted (see Growing Wheat Sprouts, page 38). Each bean *expands* and softens dramatically when *rehydrated*. ("Feel it! What makes it soft now?")

Weighing and measuring the beans before and after *absorption*, and recording the results will show the dramatic change and provide practice in handling data.

Vocabulary

*absorb to soak up

absorption the act of soaking up

embryo the form of a plant or an animal in the early stages of growth

expand to increase in size; to spread out

periodically at regular time intervals, such as every 5 minutes

rehydrate to restore water to a dried substance

*slotted having narrow openings

Materials

scales to measure ounces

pie pan in which to weigh beans

saucepan with lid

stove or hot plate

measuring cups and spoons

slotted spoon

fork and plate for each student

ingredients listed on experiment page

pencils

copy of Table 3 for each student

Discussion Questions

- How many times heavier is a rehydrated bean than a dehydrated bean? How many times bigger is the rehydrated bean?
- Where do beans get water when they grow on the plant? Where does that water go when they have been dried?
- What are some other examples of something dry absorbing something wet?
- What are two reasons for carrying dried foods when backpacking? (Would you rather carry fresh or dried apples on your back? How long will fresh foods keep?)

Related Activities

- Let cooked beans stand in a covered container until mold forms (perhaps as long as a month). Examine the mold with a magnifying glass. Discuss why mold will form on moist beans but not on dried beans.
- Learn about other dried beans (mung, kidney, pinto, garbanzo, lentil, black-eyed pea, and so on). Find recipes for cooking them. Try sprouting various beans (see Growing Wheat Sprouts, page 38).
- Compare the pods of fresh peas, lima beans, string beans, and peanuts. Open the pods, then split the beans, and find the embryos. Make comparisons.

4

Coagulation: How Does Heat Affect Protein?

Protein molecules are composed of amino acids and include nitrogen, in addition to carbon, hydrogen, and oxygen—the three elements found in carbohydrates and fats. To build and restore cells, a body needs many different kinds of amino acids, and a human body can synthesize most of these itself. About eight of the amino acids must be eaten directly because the body cannot manufacture them. Grains contain some of these eight amino acids; beans and nuts have others in various proportions. Eggs and muscle meats, such as chops and roasts, are sources of all eight essential amino acids. Milk and glandular meats are also rich in essential proteins.

Heat affects different substances in different ways. As discussed later, some substances soften when heated (see SOFTENING, page 22). But when we heat animal protein it becomes firm, or coagulated, trapping moisture as its structure solidifies. Solidified protein cannot be returned to its original soft condition. In fact, overcooking firm protein can cause it to toughen. This happens because the moisture that was trapped begins to escape, causing the protein to shrink and toughen.

Eggs are a good and inexpensive protein source and are readily available, compact, and easy to cook. They are ideal for use in the development of concepts related to protein. By hard boiling eggs, students will learn that protein coagulates when heated.

Objectives

- To introduce the characteristics of protein
- To establish the concept of coagulation
- To convey the uses of protein by chicken embryos and by the human body

Applied Skills

Motor Skills: puncturing eggshells, peeling hard-boiled eggs, mashing egg yolks, breaking raw eggs, whisking eggs, grating cheese, rolling omelet

Measuring: measuring volume and time

Estimating: estimating a half pot of water, equal parts of yolk mixture, 1/8 teaspoon

Observing: finding the blastodisc on an egg yolk, seeing air bubbles escape from boiling eggs, watching for drops of water to begin to dance on an omelet pan

Key Ideas

- Food proteins are absorbed by our bodies to build human protein.
- Protein helps build muscle, hair, blood, and other body cells.
- A chicken develops inside the egg, nurtured by the protein-rich yolk.

18

- Eggs are an excellent source of complete protein.
- Protein coagulates when heated and becomes tough if heated too long.
- Air expands when heated.

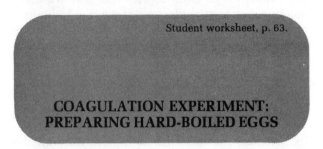

Student worksheet, p. 63.

COAGULATION EXPERIMENT: PREPARING HARD-BOILED EGGS

Break an egg into a flat dish. Find the small light-colored spot which usually rests on the top side of the *yolk*. Inside the shell of a fertilized egg, the chicken grows from this spot, called the *blastodisc*. ("What do you think the yolk is for?") Blood vessels develop here to take the *protein* from the yolk and turn it into proteins for the developing chicken. Thus, the little spot which began as a single *cell* develops into a chicken within 21 days. When eaten by humans, the yolk furnishes a good part of the recommended daily nutrients. ("You eat eggs and turn them into human proteins, such as muscle protein or hair protein.")

The space at the broad end of a fertile egg contains both air for the developing embryo and waste gas from the embryo. Even the eggs that we eat, though usually infertile, have an air space. The air expands when heated and may crack the shell as it pushes outward (see LEAVENING, page 35). A pinhole in the shell will let the air escape without causing damage.

The students can make this air hole by holding the egg firmly, without squeezing it, in the palm of the hand while pushing a pin slowly through the shell. Discuss which end of the egg to *puncture*. Or, you may want the students to discover by experiment that if the hole is made in the pointed end, part of the egg will be pushed out as air seeks to escape from the opposite end.

Allow an hour for discussion and activities centered around the boiling of the eggs. Filling a pot half full of water becomes a game if you ask the students to estimate the volume before measuring. Each student approximates half a pot of water and then checks his or her estimate with a ruler. ("How can you prove that you have half a pot of water?") Let the students discover the measuring method by themselves. If the cooking pot is 4½ in. high, let them figure out that half of 4½ is 2¼. Once the pot is on the stove, let them check the water temperature as it reaches the boiling point.

Students may take turns lowering eggs into the boiling water with a slotted spoon. Remind them to watch for escaping air bubbles. Use a clock to determine at what time the eggs will be cooked (allow 15 minutes). Discuss the reasons for rapidly cooling the eggs. Explain that plunging hot hard-boiled eggs into cold water helps prevent a dark surface from forming on the yolks and enables the shells to be removed easily.

Vocabulary

blastodisc the embryo-forming portion of an egg that is usually characterized by a small, light-colored spot

cell the smallest unit of living matter (Some very small plants and animals are made up of only one cell. Human beings are made up of billions of cells.)

*coagulate to thicken into a mass

protein a complex combination of amino acids; substance found in all living cells which helps in tissue formation and repair

puncture to make a hole with a sharp, pointed object

yolk the yellow portion of an egg in which food is stored for the chicken embryo

Materials

ruler

saucepan

stove or hot plate

safety pins for puncturing eggs

thermometer, good to above 212°F.

slotted spoon

bowl of cold water

ingredients listed on experiment page

Discussion Questions

- How does protein help the human body?
- What effect does cooking have on protein?

- What effect does over cooking have on protein?
- Does a developing chicken use cooked or raw protein?
- Which is easier to digest—cooked or raw protein? Why?
- What does half full mean?
- How does puncturing an eggshell help in boiling eggs?
- Which end of the egg should you puncture with a pin? Why?
- Why is there a pocket of gas at one end of an egg? What happens if the gas tries to escape?

Related Activities

- Discuss how chicken embryos use protein to build cells.
- Examine eggshells and egg membranes for pores. Discuss osmosis, the passage of a substance through a semipermeable wall.
- Study photographs and drawings from science magazines and other sources that show the chicken growing in the egg.

Student worksheet, p. 64.

COAGULATION EXPERIMENT: MAKING DEVILED EGGS

Protein builds and strengthens every part of the body. The value of eggs in nourishing human cells lies not only in their concentrated, complete protein, but also in the *vitamins* and *minerals* they contain. Vitamin A is needed to build an enzyme that helps the eyes to see and helps to keep skin and hair healthy and lustrous. It also enables the tissues lining the body cavities to produce mucus which protects them from bacteria. Vitamin B_2, or riboflavin, is needed for another enzyme that helps maintain healthy eyes and skin. Iron, a mineral, is used in the formation of hemoglobin, the substance in red blood cells that delivers oxygen to the cells of the body. Another mineral, calcium, is used in building bones and teeth. Phosphorus and potassium are two other essential minerals. Phosphorus works along with calcium to regulate cell activity. Potassium contributes to heart and muscle tone and helps to maintain blood sugar level, thus preventing fatigue.

If the students mention the high cholesterol in eggs and other animal foods, you might point out that the controversy concerning cholesterol continues. It has been established that we manufacture our own cholesterol if we don't obtain it from food and that human body processes require a certain amount of it. It is only excessive consumption of foods containing cholesterol that creates problems.

When they remove the shells of the eggs in the experiment, the students can examine the egg *membranes* and notice their strength and elasticity. Discuss the fact that air passes through the membrane and shell for use by the developing chick.

Vocabulary

membrane thin layer of tough, elastic tissue that lines the eggshell and covers the yolk, through which gases and fluids can pass back and forth as needed

mineral a substance found in the earth that is a necessary ingredient of plant and animal cells

vitamin a substance made in living plants and animals that has a special use in promoting growth and health

Materials

reamer (juice extractor)

3 forks, knives, and small spoons

measuring spoons

shallow dish or glass pie pan

serving plate for eggs

ingredients listed on experiment page

Discussion Questions

- Why are eggs an important food?
- How do egg membranes look and feel?
- What do egg membranes do?
- Why did we sprinkle the paprika and not mash it into the egg yolk?
- Why did we divide the mashed eggs into sixths?
- What flavors do you taste in the deviled eggs?
- What textures do the deviled eggs have?

Related Activities

- Discuss protein as it is used by the human body to build cells.
- Study complementary proteins in plant sources (for example, grains with beans) as well as complete proteins in animal sources.
- Investigate the functions of protein in bodily processes.
- Learn about the sources and uses of paprika.
- Exchange different ideas about other seasonings for deviled eggs (see SENSORY PERCEPTION, page 42).

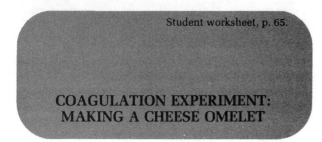

Student worksheet, p. 65.

COAGULATION EXPERIMENT: MAKING A CHEESE OMELET

Brought up in America on fluffy omelets, which started with beating yolks and whites separately as in making a soufflé, I thought that the celebrated French omelet must be even fluffier. My visions of airy omelets were deflated when I had my first Parisian omelet, which is actually like an egg pancake, that is folded in half, as in the following experiment.

Whichever way it is prepared, the omelet is a popular food that demonstrates the coagulation of eggs as it occurs. Though a mystique exists about the best omelet pan, one with sloping sides fulfills the main requirement. Oiling and salting the hot pan will prevent the omelet from sticking.

Let the students read the entire recipe, practice the motions, and then choose specific tasks. Advance planning is vital to complete the quick sequence of steps required in making a good omelet.

Discuss the reasons for *whisking* the omelet with a fork. The action not only blends the eggs into a smooth mixture, but also adds air to help lighten the mass (See LEAVENING, page 35).

Vocabulary

grate to cut a substance into shreds by rubbing it over a rough surface

whisk to whip quickly and lightly

Materials

grater (optional)

mixing bowl

measuring spoons

medium frying pan with sloping sides

stove or hot plate

fork to whisk the omelet

spatula

serving plate

plate and fork for each student

ingredients listed on experiment page

Discussion Questions

- How does coating a frying pan with salt and oil help in preparing an omelet?
- Why does the omelet fluff up when heated?
- What does heat do to the egg protein?
- If you returned a bit of omelet to the pan to cook, would it become softer or tougher? Why?

Related Activities

- Return a bit of the omelet to the frying pan for additional cooking. Notice how the omelet toughens with additional heat on the protein.
- Find other omelet recipes that vary omelet fillings to include herbs and spices (see SENSORY PERCEPTION, page 42), stewed tomatoes, or sautéed mushrooms.
- Make a fluffier omelet by beating the whites separately and then folding them into the beaten yolks (see Making Apple Puffs, page 36).
- Make boiled custard to show that eggs can thicken liquids in which they are cooked.

5

Softening: How Does Heat Affect Cellulose?

Many people resist vegetables when confronted by a mass of overcooked and discolored pulp. However, when they cut into a crisp head of purple cabbage or slice a bright, fresh carrot they are able to enjoy the colorful beauty and firm texture. With the students, explore the way vegetables grow. Study their intricate designs. Manipulate grinders, graters, mashers, and other tools which transform vegetables in interesting ways. Compare the textures of vegetables before and after cooking them. Sample properly cooked crisp and nutritious vegetables rather than overcooked, mushy ones. Try some exotic vegetables and compare them with familiar ones.

In contrast to the effects of heat on protein (see COAGULATION, page 18), this unit will show what heat does to cellulose in vegetables. While they are growing, fruit and vegetable cells are firm and the tissues, crisp. Each juicy, microscopic cell is surrounded by a strong wall of cellulose, and the cellulose fibers support most parts of the plant. Heat weakens the cellulose, causing the fruit or vegetable to loose its stiffness and become limp.

Raw vegetables are good for us because stiff cellulose acts as roughage to stimulate the digestive tract and because the vitamins and minerals are still intact. Overcooking destroys vitamins and minerals. But since it is easier to eat cooked vegetables, we can consume many more in the cooked than in the raw state. Thus, by sheer volume, it is possible to get more of most nutrients in cooked vegetables—as long as they aren't subjected to prolonged soaking and heating.

Objectives

- To identify vegetables as one of six basic parts of a plant (roots, stems, leaves, flowers, fruits or seeds)
- To understand that cellulose is a stiffening material in plants
- To explore the phenomenon of heat softening cellulose, yet hardening protein
- To compare the various textures and nutritional values of raw vegetables with cooked vegetables
- To determine the nutritional benefits of eating vegetables
- To understand the important role vegetables play in stimulating digestion
- To introduce starch as a form in which nutrients are stored

Applied Skills

Motor Skills: chopping and slicing vegetables, mashing potatoes, using a pastry bag (optional)

Measuring: measuring volume, and interpreting guide marks on a stick of butter

Observing: noting shapes, textures, patterns, colors, flavors

Key Ideas

- Vegetables come from parts of plants: roots, stems, leaves, flowers, fruits, or seeds.

- Cellulose is the supporting structure (stiffening material) of vegetables.

- We cook vegetables to break down the cellulose and make the vegetables more digestible and to enable us to eat them in greater quantity.

- We eat vegetables raw because they are crisp and juicy and have more vitamins and minerals than after they are cooked.

- Vegetables are good for us because they have vitamins and minerals and because the roughage from cellulose stimulates digestion.

Student worksheet, p. 66.

SOFTENING EXPERIMENT: MAKING A COOKED VEGETABLE PLATTER

Vegetables defined in a dietary sense include many plant parts, and the "scientific" eater can focus precisely on what part he or she is eating. When we think about it, six various parts of a plant might be edible: roots, stems, leaves, flowers, fruits, or seeds. ("What part of this plant do we eat? Do we eat the leaves of a corn, lettuce, or carrot plant?")

Cut pictures from a vegetable seed catalog. Mount them on cards and make a corresponding name card identifying each one. Make a game of categorizing the vegetables as roots, stems, leaves, flowers, fruits, or seeds.

Even though we don't usually eat the whole of any one plant, all six parts of it contain *cellulose*, which supports the parts as they grow. We often cook vegetables to soften the cellulose, which is a substance that cannot be *digested* by humans. However, it is valuable to us as *roughage*, which keeps the digestive tract active and stimulates digestion of all foods.

Find bright, fresh vegetables that represent the six different parts of a plant and that demonstrate as much variety in color and shape as possible. The recipe gives suggestions, but it is more creative and fun to let a good produce market inspire you.

Vegetables contain vitamins (especially A and C), minerals (especially *calcium* and *iron*), and other valuable *nutrients*. Wash the vegetables thoroughly in cold water, working quickly so as not to soak out the nutrients. Shake off or quickly dry the vegetables. If you steam vegetables in a rack above boiling water, you avoid prolonged soaking and overcooking, and you help the vegetables retain their shape, color, and nutrients. Your colorful, nutritious array will look very appetizing.

While you are eating, discuss what part of the plant you are tasting and compare the cooked vegetable with the same one in the raw state.

Vocabulary

cellulose a complex sugar-related substance, the main component of the cell walls and fibers in plants

calcium a soft, white metal essential to human and animal nutrition; found in the bones and teeth

digest to change food into a form that can be absorbed by the body

iron a metal essential to human nutrition; found in largest amounts in red blood cells

nutrient any substance needed for life and growth, such as protein, carbohydrate, fat, vitamin, or mineral

roughage indigestible substances, such as plant fibers, that stimulate the digestive tract to push its contents through the intestines

Materials

3 or more serrated knives

large saucepan with lid

steaming rack (optional)

hot plate or stove

ruler

slotted spoon

fork and plate for each student

ingredients listed on experiment page

Discussion Questions

- What parts of plants do we eat? Give examples.

- Why do we eat vegetables?

- How does heat change vegetables?

- What is cellulose?
- How does eating raw vegetables help us to digest other food?
- What new vegetables have you learned about?
- Which vegetables do you prefer cooked, and which raw?

Related Activities

- Take a trip to a produce market where students can identify new vegetables. Purchase some to try out on your vegetable platter.
- Make a raw vegetable salad, using carrots, celery, lettuce, cauliflower, peas, and tomatoes to represent each of the six parts of a plant.
- Do library research on the histories of familiar and unfamiliar vegetables.
- Learn about the vitamin and mineral contents of specific vegetables.
- Find out how plant fibers are used in making rope, cloth, paper, and other products.
- Play "Concentration" with vegetable cards of one color and corresponding word cards of another color. Spread the cards down on a table. A player turns over one card of each color. If the name card corresponds to the vegetable card, the player keeps the cards. If not, the cards must be replaced to their positions on the table, and the next player takes a turn.

Student worksheet, p. 67.

SOFTENING EXPERIMENT: MAKING TWICE-BAKED POTATOES

The potato was developed and used by Indians in South America. Spanish explorers returning from their search for gold in South America introduced the potato to Europe. Europe gradually adopted it, and it is now the most widely used vegetable in the Western Hemisphere. Many varieties have been bred, including the huge, dry Idaho baking potatoes and the moist New England potatoes.

A potato crop can give more nourishment per acre than almost any other crop. The *starch* in a potato is in an easily digestible form, and protein is also present, especially next to the skin. Potatoes contain many of the B vitamins as well as vitamin C and the minerals iron and potassium. This vegetable grows well in cool climates where other vegetables will not grow and also stores very well for extended periods of time.

Potatoes are not roots. They are the swollen ends of the plant's underground stems, called *tubers*. The starch which they contain has been stored by the plant for future use (see THICKENING, page 26).

For its nourishment, a plant makes sugar through the process of *photosynthesis*. The excess sugar molecules ($C_6H_{12}O_6$) are changed into starch ($C_6H_{10}O_5$). Since starch is insoluble, it is the ideal form in which to store nutrients for future use. The plant turns the starch back into sugar when it needs nourishment for growth and maintenance. We turn starch back into sugar when we digest it.

Another way a plant uses starch is to make cellulose. Sugar, starch, and cellulose are all *carbohydrates*, but cellulose cannot be changed back into sugar by the plant or digested by humans. In the process of roasting a potato—a process which resembles that of popping corn (see Making Popcorn, page 27)—air and vapor between the potato cells expand, and heat forces the cells apart. This expansion, in addition to the cellulose softening, is an additional factor in the softening of many vegetables when they are cooked.

Twice-baked potatoes are delicious, and they are fun to make. Eat the crusty skin, because the protein lies close to it. The value of this protein is enhanced by supplementary amino acids when you drink a glass of milk with your potato. Or, you can top your baked potatoes with grated cheese for a tasty, nutritious treat.

Vocabulary

carbohydrate a class of foods that includes sugars, starches, and cellulose, all composed of carbon, hydrogen, and oxygen

photosynthesis the changes made by the green leaves of plants when they take carbon dioxide (CO_2) and water (H_2O) and turn them into carbohydrates, using the energy from light

starch a powdery carbohydrate stored by plants

tuber the thickened part of an underground stem from which new plants grow

Materials

oven

serrated knife

cutting board

measuring spoons

small spoons for scooping

food mill or potato masher

mixing bowl for potato pulp

pastry bag with fluting attachment (optional)

shallow pan

knife, fork, and plate for each student

ingredients listed on experiment page

Discussion Questions

- What part of the plant is a potato?
- What is a tuber?
- How is potato starch formed and stored by the plant?
- How is the starch used by a potato plant?
- Why is the potato such a valuable vegetable?

Related Activities

- Plant a section of a sprouting potato 4 in. deep in average soil. Keep it cool and moist.
- Pull up a potato plant to observe the roots and the tubers.
- Learn how sweet potatoes are similar to, and different from, white potatoes.
- Read about the famous potato famine that occurred in Ireland.
- Find out how the cellulose in grass is used by some animals for nourishment.
- Enjoy a print of van Gogh's painting *The Potato Eaters*.

6

Thickening: How Does Heat Affect Starch?

Try to dissolve some flour in a glass of water while dissolving sugar in another glass. Even though the molecular formulas of sugar, ($C_6H_{12}O_6$) and starch ($C_6H_{10}O_5$) are similar, starch molecules cannot be dissolved in water. Thus, they do not diffuse among water molecules the way sugar molecules do, although you will see that they can be suspended for a while (see DISSOLUTION, page 5).

To introduce the characteristics of starch, perform two simple experiments. Soak a handful of rolled oats in cold water overnight. The oats won't dissolve, but they will swell considerably. Also, cook a spoonful of flour in a cup of water and observe the sticky mass that results.

Like cellulose (see SOFTENING, page 22), starch is a carbohydrate whose nutritional value is locked within tough cellular walls. But, unlike cellulose, starch can be digested by humans.

The $H_{10}O_5$ portion of the starch molecule contains hydrogen and oxygen in the same proportion (two to one) as does water (H_2O). You drive water out of the starch molecules by burning, and the carbon is left as a charred black substance.

The human body turns starch into glucose ($C_6H_{12}O_6$). It then takes carbon from the glucose to use as the fuel that combines with oxygen in metabolism: $C + O_2 = CO_2$ (carbon dioxide), and the production of energy. In other words, during metabolism, the carbon in glucose is oxidized (see OXIDATION, page 9), producing heat, which is used as energy, and CO_2, which is eventually exhaled.

Tincture of iodine is an indicator of starch. Iodine will turn starch, and *only* starch, purple upon contact. Keep the iodine separate from the food products: IODINE IS POISONOUS. After you are through eating, test some remaining food for starch content.

Objectives

- To teach the properties of starch, which is also a carbohydrate
- To show how the bursting and thickening characteristics of starch are utilized in cooking
- To review the concept that plants store starch
- To introduce various grains that contain starch

Applied Skills

Motor Skills: agitating a pan, grating cheese, chopping celery and nuts, stirring and whisking mixtures

Measuring: measurement of volume, time, and size of slices

Observing: noting consistencies of foods, seeing the effects of iodine on starch, listening to corn popping

26

Key Ideas

- Starch is a carbohydrate.
- Starch is made and stored by plants.
- Starch molecules are tough-coated granules with soft centers.
- Water softens the tough outer layers of the starch granule.
- Heat causes the tough outer layers of the starch granule to open.
- The center of a starch granule absorbs water and becomes sticky, resulting in a thickening effect.
- A coating of oil keeps starch granules from sticking to each other.
- Enzymes in saliva can digest starch.

Student worksheet, p. 68.

THICKENING EXPERIMENT: MAKING POPCORN

If you soak thinly sliced potatoes in water for a day, a fine white sediment will settle from them. This sediment is starch—minute, powdery granules in which several tough layers cover a soft center. Water softens these layers, and heating the water causes each granule to absorb a large amount of water. Additional heat causes the granules to rupture and the soft centers to spill out. This soft material has a sticky quality and tends to cling together in a mass.

Starch can be changed in another way. Chew an unsweetened cracker or some grains of wheat for a few minutes. Suddenly you will sense a sweet taste in your mouth. Starch $(C_6H_{10}O_5)$ has become glucose $(C_6H_{12}O_6)$, a simple sugar. The enzymes in your saliva have digested the starch and changed it to a simple sugar. It is then ready for absorption into the body even before it reaches the stomach.

When we make popcorn, starch is changed by extreme heat. Starch and moisture are stored in corn *kernels* by the corn plant. Sudden high heat changes the moisture inside the kernel into water vapor that explodes the starch. The exploded starch puffs out around the husk.

Popcorn plants are somewhat smaller than regular corn plants. After maturing, the ears are allowed to dry. The kernels harden on the ears and are then rubbed off for popping. If not popped, they become the seeds for new popcorn plants. ("What will the stored starch in the kernel be used for as the seed starts to grow?").

Be careful at the stove. *Agitation* and popping must be confined to the corn. Agitated students tend to get burned.

Paint some iodine (POISON!) on a popped corn kernel to see the instant reaction to the starch. Then test bread, potato, sugar, butter, and hard-boiled egg white for starch.

Vocabulary

agitate to move rapidly

kernel the seed or grain of a cereal plant

Materials

medium saucepan with lid

stove or hot plate

measuring cup and spoons

ingredients listed on experiment page

Discussion Questions

- What is starch?
- What does heat do to the starch in corn kernels?
- Why do you need to agitate the pan while popping corn?
- How does it feel to bite popped corn? To bite an unpopped kernel?
- What do you taste when you chew popcorn for five minutes? Why?

Related Activities

- Before it is popped, cut open a kernel of corn to see the starch inside.
- Plant some popcorn kernels.
- Boil some popped popcorn for 20 minutes. See and feel the fine white starch in the water.
- Soak grated or thinly sliced potatoes overnight. Examine the fine white starch which settles to the bottom.
- Find out how postage stamp glue is made from roasted starch.

Student worksheet, p. 69.

THICKENING EXPERIMENT: MAKING POLENTA

Tubers yield starch beneath the soil (see Making Twice-Baked Potatoes, page 24), but the tops of plants, especially the grains of grasses, also produce starch above the soil. Corn, or maize, was the first grain successfully grown in America. It saved the lives of the settlers when wheat and other grains they had brought from Europe failed to grow. They found that corn had a short growing season and grew strong in the American climate, so they adopted it from the Indians and learned to like its flavor.

In the United States, new strains of wheat have been developed to match our climate so that we can now raise and use this grain. In Mexico, most people are still dependent on corn, and it is basic to the daily diet.

Ears of corn become sweet and juicy as they mature and some varieties are bred to be eaten at this stage ("How do you like your corn on the cob?"). Most corn, though, is bred to dry well on the stalk, so that it keeps well as livestock feed. Corn is also used for making cornstarch and corn syrup. We can eat dried corn in the form of hominy, cornmeal, or corn flour. The *germ* is often removed from the kernel to keep it from spoiling and is used to make corn oil, leaving the starchy *endosperm* (see Growing Wheat Sprouts, page 38). On the other hand, we may eat the entire grain in the form of "water ground" cornmeal, which is made from complete corn kernels that are crushed between flat stone wheels.

Polenta is the name for a cornmeal mush popularized by the Italians. ("Watch as you stir the watery mixture over heat. What is happening to the cornmeal and water to make it thicken?") Swelling grains of cornstarch absorb enough water to give the mixture a mushy *consistency*. The cornmeal will absorb more water as it continues to cook in the double boiler. ("What would happen if you cooked the polenta too long?")

Compare the *textures* of uncooked and boiled cornmeal. Can you notice a difference in taste? Test it for starch with iodine (POISON!) away from the eating area.

Vocabulary

consistency the degree of firmness of a substance or of a mixture

endosperm the starchy part of a seed which the developing plant uses for nourishment

germ the embryo of a cereal grain

texture the quality of a substance that gives it a characteristic feel and appearance (smooth, grainy, soft, hard, and so on)

Materials

double boiler with lid

stove or hot plate

measuring cups and spoons

mixing spoon

grater

serving spoon

bowl and spoon for each student

ingredients listed on experiment page

for polenta (optional): frying pan, oil, and spatula; fork and plate for each student

Discussion Questions

- What happens to corn on the cob when it ripens beyond the eating stage?
- What are the parts of a corn kernel?
- How is cornmeal made?
- What happens when cornmeal is put in water?
- What happens to cornmeal when it is heated?
- How does cornmeal act as a thickener?
- What would happen if you didn't stir the cornmeal while it was beginning to thicken?

Related Activities

- Learn about Mexican dishes made with corn tortillas.
- Find a recipe for Indian Pudding, which is cornmeal baked with milk, molasses, and spices, and often topped with ice cream.
- Find out how corn syrup is made from cornstarch.
- Read about the "cornhusking bees" that occurred during colonial days.

- Investigate the uses of corncobs, corn stalks, and leaves.
- Find out how cornflakes are made.
- Cook oatmeal and watch it swell and thicken. Add some raisins and let them cook until they also swell.
- Mix flour and water to make a paste, as a simple demonstration that water makes starch sticky.

Student worksheet, p. 70.

THICKENING EXPERIMENT: MAKING CREAMED CELERY

Americans daily consume tons of breakfast foods, bread, and other bakery goods made from wheat flour. Whole wheat flour, ground from the entire grain of wheat, is sometimes used, but more often white flour is used. White flour is made from only one part of the wheat grain, the endosperm, after the bran and germ have been removed. In addition, we also use the separated parts of the wheat grain in various ways. Wheat germ is used for oil; bran is used for animal feed; and starch from the endosperm is used for paste, for stiffening cloth, and as a filler and binder in baking powder.

In the kitchen, wheat flour is used for the stiffening qualities of its starch as well as for its nourishment. We have already seen that starch will not dissolve, but it can be suspended in liquid and this mixture will thicken with heat. Making a cream sauce—basic to the art of cooking—not only illustrates the thickening characteristic of starch, but also makes use of oil to keep starch grains from sticking to each other as they heat in milk.

In this experiment, first coat the grains of wheat flour with butter to make a roux (pronounced "roo"). A roux is a cooked mixture of flour and oil used as a thickening agent in soups and sauces. Coated with oil, the starch grains in a roux will not cling together and cook to a lumpy mass; instead, they remain evenly separated while they absorb liquid and expand, making a smooth sauce.

Vocabulary

bran the tough outer layer of a cereal grain which protects the endosperm

*stalk the main stem of a plant, that portion of a plant which supports other parts

Materials

2 medium saucepans, one with a lid

steaming rack (optional)

stove or hot plate

measuring cups and spoons

wire whisk

serrated knives

ruler

cutting board

slotted spoon

serving spoon

fork and plate for each student

ingredients listed on experiment page

Discussion Questions

- Why did you put the flour into melted butter to start the sauce?
- Why is it better to use a wire whisk than a spoon when making cream sauce?
- How would you make a thicker sauce for the creamed celery?
- What steps might you follow to make gravy from the fat and juices of meat?

Related Activities

- Try making a cream sauce without adding oil. Discuss the reasons for the results.
- Read about the growing of wheat in ancient history. For example, research the Biblical story of Joseph in Egypt.
- Learn how tough wheat plants have been developed from tender grasses.
- Plant a variety of grains (oats, barley, rye, corn, and wheat) and observe the growing plants. Study and compare the mature heads of the plants.
- Plant beans and compare the bean plants with the grain plants. Also compare the mature heads of grain plants with bean pods.

7

Separation: How Does Beating Affect the Ingredients?

An eggbeater is fun to use and can yield a variety of interesting results. From fluid oil and egg yolk, you can whip up a stiff mayonnaise. You can change transparent egg white into a fluffy, opaque foam. And you can transform liquid cream into a soft, delicious heap, or into a pile of butter surrounded by a thin pool of milk.

In scientific terms, you have made an emulsion (mayonnaise); straightened the curled-up molecules of protein (meringue); and caused the drops of fat in cream to coalesce (whipped cream, butter). In each case, you have changed the form of the original substance into a new one. The instrument for change is the same eggbeater, yet with each of the three substances a different physical change has taken place.

The following experiments demonstrate these physical changes and suggest ways to use the products. Keep in mind that beating can produce three kinds of separations: (1) the separation of a substance into small drops and their distribution throughout a different substance (emulsifying oil in egg yolk to produce mayonnaise, or cream in milk to yield homogenized milk); (2) the separation of the particles of one substance from another by stretching them out (unrolling curled-up protein molecules in egg white to make a structure for trapping air); and (3) the separation of the particles of one substance from those of another by causing the particles of the first substance to coalesce (the joining of fat particles in cream to make butter).

Table 4 is reproduced in a duplicatable copy at the back of this book. Distribute a copy of it to each student before the separation experiments are performed. The table will serve as an easy reference for the events observed in the course of the experiments.

Objectives

- To observe the physical changes produced by beating various substances
- To convey the nature of these physical changes as being three different separation processes
- To strengthen an awareness of the sources and nature of vegetable oils, butter, and cream
- To broaden the scope of information about eggs

Applied Skills

Motor Skills: separating egg yolk from egg white, squeezing lemon, adding ingredients slowly, beating, sifting

Measuring: measuring volume

Observing: watching oil separate from other liquids, testing stiffness of whipped cream and beaten egg white, listening for the gritty sound of undissolved sugar in beaten egg white

Coordinating movements: one person beating while another adds ingredients

Key Ideas

- When oil is beaten, it can be suspended, or emulsified, in another liquid.

- When oil is beaten into liquid egg yolk, each drop of oil becomes coated with egg and is separated from the other oil drops.

- When egg whites are beaten, molecules of protein are unrolled, or stretched out, and air is beaten among them.

- Cream contains fat, which is similar to oil.

- When cream is whipped, the fat drops join together, or coalesce, and trap both the separated milk and the air that is beaten into the cream.

- When whipped cream is beaten for a prolonged time, the fat drops join together in a solid mass as butter, squeezing out the milk and the air.

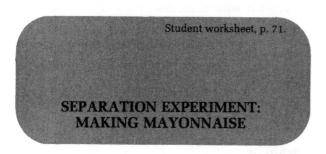

Student worksheet, p. 71.

SEPARATION EXPERIMENT: MAKING MAYONNAISE

Cooking oil is pressed from grains, seeds, and nuts. Oil cannot be dissolved in water, but it can be temporarily suspended in it if you separate it into small drops by agitating it. If you coat these drops with egg yolk, or with some other *emulsifying agent*, you can maintain their separation and they will remain suspended.

In a jar, shake together some oil and water. Watch them separate. ("Which is lighter—oil or water?") Since no adhesive force exists between the molecules of oil and water, the oil does not dissolve (see DISSOLUTION, page 5). Instead, the *cohesive* force of oil unites the oil particles, and the cohesive force of water unites the water particles.

As a control for the mayonnaise experiment, you should try beating oil slowly into a bowl of water or lemon juice and vinegar. ("What happens to the drops of oil after we stop beating the mixture?") When this attempt to *emulsify* oil fails,

proceed with the mayonnaise experiment. Establish the egg as the emulsifying agent, which keeps the oil from *coalescing* into one mass. (If the mayonnaise begins to curdle, it means that the oil is being added too fast and is coalescing. Begin again in a clean bowl with another beaten egg yolk, adding the curdled mixture to it very slowly.)

When the experiment is finished, wash the greasy mayonnaise bowl in hot water without soap or detergent. ("Feel it.") Now wash it with detergent. ("Feel it again.") Soap is an emulsifier of oils. The soap coats the drops of fat, separating them from each other and distributing them through the soap mixture, which can then be washed away.

Vocabulary

coalesce to come together into a mass

cohesive wanting or tending to stick to other like things or particles

emulsify to separate a liquid into such fine drops that each drop can float separately throughout another liquid

emulsifying agent a substance that coats the drops of another substance so that the drops can remain separated throughout a mixture

Materials

eggbeater

2 bowls; one a small, deep mixing bowl

reamer (juice extractor)

measuring cups and spoons

containers to store egg whites and mayonnaise

refrigerator for ingredients

ingredients listed on experiment page (allow extra amounts)

Discussion Questions

- What happens to oil when you beat it into water? What happens to the water?

- What happens to oil when it is beaten with egg yolk?

- Can mayonnaise be separated into egg and oil again? Why or why not?

- How does emulsifying compare with dissolving? How does soap help to wash away oil?

Related Activities

- Make French dressing with oil, vinegar, garlic, salt, pepper, and a little honey and tarragon. Shake it to suspend the oil.

- Make a raw vegetable salad using the six parts of plants (see Making a Cooked Vegetable Platter, page 23). Toss with French dressing or top with mayonnaise.

- Crush peanuts and other nuts and grains in a brown paper bag. Notice the oil which is absorbed by the bag.

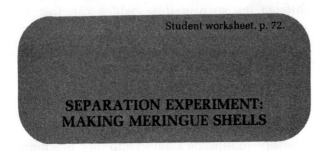

Student worksheet. p. 72.

SEPARATION EXPERIMENT: MAKING MERINGUE SHELLS

The white of an egg is the *albumen*. It surrounds the yolk in four layers and contains half the protein of the egg, some of the minerals and vitamins, a large quantity of water, and a little fat. The innermost layer of albumen, the *chalaza*, is twisted at each end of the yolk and is attached by these twisted ends to an outer membrane. Acting as a swing which supports the yolk, the chalaza allows the yolk to rock inside the egg but prevents it from floating freely.

Poach an egg in gently boiling water; watch the albumen become opaque and white as it coagulates. Because it also coagulates around impurities, albumen is used to settle out fine grounds from boiled coffee.

Albumen (or a similar protein, albumin) is also used in industry for collecting impurities. To manufacture cream of tartar, for example, albumen is added to wine sediment. The egg white coats and separates the colored matter, leaving the white, powdery cream of tartar which you may have on your spice shelf.

Cream of tartar's acidity helps to maintain the foam produced by beating egg whites. Before egg whites are beaten, they contain curled-up molecules of protein. Agitation *denatures* the molecules by unrolling them until they resemble stretched-out fibers. Still attracted to each other by cohesion, the threadlike molecules form a three-dimensional network. In this structure, the molecules trap the air beaten into the egg white. When cooked, the molecules become rigid, making the structure permanent.

After beating the egg whites into a foam, start sprinkling sugar on them. ("What makes the sugar dissolve?") As you continue beating, you have two sticky substances (egg white and concentrated sugar solution) trapping the air that is being forced into the mixture.

If you bake meringue in a hot oven, it will be chewy and tough (see COAGULATION, page 18). If you bake it slowly, it will be tender and crumbly. The protein becomes firm, without toughening, when baked at a low temperature. The moisture turns into steam, expands, and then evaporates, swelling the meringue in the process (see LEAVENING, page 35).

Vocabulary

albumen the white portion of an egg which protects the yolk and developing chick and provides it with moisture

chalaza the inner layer of albumen which supports the yolk

denature to change a substance in such a way that it cannot be returned to its original state

*sift to break up the lumps in a substance by forcing it through a sieve or strainer

Materials

mixing bowl (not plastic)

eggbeater

cookie sheet

heavy brown paper to cover cookie sheet

butter to grease paper

oven

sifter

measuring cups and spoons

large spoon

small spoon for each student

spatula

ingredients listed on experiment page

Discussion Questions

- Why do egg whites get foamy when you beat them?

- Why does air beaten into egg whites at room temperature expand the whites more than air beaten into cold egg whites?
- What makes sugar dissolve in egg whites?
- Why do you add cream of tartar when beating egg whites?
- What makes meringue expand in the oven?
- What makes meringue crisp?

Related Activities

- Poach eggs in boiling water and observe how the albumen coagulates.
- Boil muddy water, adding beaten egg white to clear it.
- Add a little vinegar instead of cream of tartar to the egg white when beating.
- Make a soft meringue to cover a pudding or pie by using much less sugar than in the meringue shell recipe.
- Make a facial by spreading a little egg white on your face. The albumen sticks to your face, the moisture evaporates, and the egg white shrinks, tightening your skin.
- Learn how eggs are formed in a hen's body.
- Study fish eggs and snake eggs to see if they have albumen.

Student worksheet, p. 73.

SEPARATION EXPERIMENT: MAKING WHIPPED CREAM

Fat drops are distributed throughout milk as it comes from the cow. If milk is allowed to settle, the fat will rise to float on top, as oil does on water, because it is lighter. At a dairy plant, milk is often homogenized in a process that breaks the fat into such tiny drops that they stay in suspension, forming an emulsion.

Cream for whipping is skimmed from the top of milk that has not been homogenized. A thin coating of milk still clings to each drop of fat. Beating cream separates the fat particles from their milky coating so that drops of fat gravitate towards each other, *cohere*, and form larger drops. Air is forced between these formations of fat, by beating. If you continue beating, the fat coalesces into a single large mass, squeezing out the air and separating itself from the liquid. Thus, by *churning*, you produce a solid and a liquid: butter and *buttermilk*.

The whipped cream made in this experiment can be used as a topping. Fill the meringue shells made in the preceding experiment with the fresh fruit prepared earlier (see Watching Air Discolor Fresh Fruit, page 10). Crown the fruit-filled shells with the whipped cream. (No sugar is added to the cream because the meringue shells are very sweet.)

Vocabulary

buttermilk the sour liquid left after butter has been churned from milk or cream; a thick milk commercially produced from skim milk by the addition of certain bacteria

churn to agitate milk or cream in order to separate the fat, or butter, from it

cohere to unite as a result of the attraction of like molecules to each other

Materials

eggbeater

small, deep mixing bowl

measuring cup and spoons

ingredients listed on experiment page

Discussion Questions

- What happens to cream as you beat it?
- Why does the cream take up more space in the bowl after you have whipped it?
- Why will cream turn to butter if you beat it a long time?

Related Activities

- Visit a dairy farm and plant.
- Learn how the cow's body processes grass (cellulose) to make milk (protein).
- Find out how much milk an average cow yields in one day.

- Investigate the food value of milk.
- Learn about the human body's need for vitamin D and calcium and investigate sources of each.
- Read about Louis Pasteur and why milk is pasteurized.
- Find out how much butter can be made from the milk of one cow.
- Make butter and buttermilk.
- Learn about the composition of churned buttermilk and compare it with cultured buttermilk.

- Study the list of ingredients on a can of artificial "whipped cream."

- Make ice cream by whipping cream and folding it into mashed bananas which have been frozen to a mush and beaten.

- Compare the whipping of cream to the practice of beating ice cream as it freezes. The process distributes the fat throughout the liquid, making an emulsion so that large ice crystals won't form in the ice cream.

8

Leavening: What Makes Batter Rise?

Leaven means "to make something rise." A leavening agent does this by producing or distributing a gas within a mixture. Yeast, baking soda, baking powder, and egg whites can all be leavening agents. Active yeast gives off carbon dioxide bubbles. Acid added to baking soda makes it fizz as carbon dioxide is released. When egg whites are beaten, bubbles of air are incorporated into the mass (see SEPARATION, page 30). All these bubbles expand when heated, pushing against whatever material surrounds them and causing dough, batter, or meringue to rise.

A simple demonstration will provide an important reference point for the experiments in this unit. Stretch a balloon over the opening of an empty half gallon vinegar jug to watch the effect of gas expanding when heated. Put the jug in a pan of water and heat the water slowly over a burner. The warming air in the jug will soon begin to blow up the balloon. A used balloon is the least resistant; if a new balloon is used, air is apt to escape along its edges. But even if air leaks out, the experiment will prove a point; for, as the jug cools, the balloon will be sucked inside so as to fill the space left by the escaped air. If you refrigerate the jug for a few hours, or surround it with ice, the results will be even more spectacular.

The expansion and contraction of the balloon is another example of the effect temperature has on molecules (see DISSOLUTION, page 5). Air is composed of freely moving molecules of gases: nitrogen (about 80 percent), oxygen (about 20 percent), and other gases, such as argon, carbon dioxide, neon, hydrogen, and helium, in very small amounts. Heat speeds up the activity of the gas molecules, increasing the rate at which they bombard the balloon confining them. They exert more pressure on the rubber, and push it outward. Since chilling slows down molecular activity, pressure by the gas molecules on the rubber is decreased. The balloon is sucked back into the jug just enough to equalize the air pressure on the inside and outside of the balloon.

This concept applies to all of the batters in the leavening experiments, whether the active gas is air or carbon dioxide. When bubbles of gas are distributed throughout a batter and then heated, each bubble pushes outward on the batter around it, making the batter fluffy. The heat also acts on the protein in the milk, eggs, and flour, stiffening them around the gas bubbles (see COAGULATION, page 18). Thus, even after the gas escapes, the firm structure of coagulated protein maintains the spaces which the gas bubbles formed.

The term batter indicates a flowing mass which is stirred or beaten and used for making cakes, muffins, and pancakes. Dough is a thicker mass which can be worked by hand and used for making breads and pastry. Leavening agents are used to make both batters and doughs.

Objectives

- To demonstrate how leavening agents act
- To foster understanding of chemical change and of single-cell growth
- To explain how the concept of molecular activity applies to gases
- To introduce the various characteristics of a wheat grain
- To teach how gluten contributes to the leavening process

Applied Skills

Motor Skills: grating apples, sifting flour, cracking and beating eggs, rubbing wheat kernels and blowing off the chaff, stirring batter, folding in egg whites, greasing a hot griddle, spooning batter onto a griddle, turning over pancakes

Computing: dividing a recipe in half, finding how to measure ½ tablespoon, comparing data in a table

Measuring: measuring volume and diameter, estimating length of wheat sprouts

Observing: comparing the reactions of soda and yeast, watching for drops of water to begin to dance on a griddle, tasting pancakes to compare flavors and textures

Key Ideas

- Air bubbles can be beaten into egg whites.
- Acid reacts with baking soda to produce carbon dioxide, a gas.
- Sugar fosters the growth of yeast cells, which give off carbon dioxide as they live and multiply.
- Gas bubbles can be trapped in batter to provide a leavening effect.
- Gas expands when it is heated because the activity of the molecules increases.
- Wheat grain is the seed of a plant and is grown, cut, threshed, separated, and ground to make wheat flour.
- The gluten in flour holds dough together as it rises.
- Wheat germ is the part of the seed from which the root and stem of a new plant grow.

LEAVENING EXPERIMENT: MAKING APPLE PUFFS

Student worksheet, p. 74.

An "eggbeater" is a common kitchen utensil with rotary blades, but it also is the slang for a helicopter. ("Have you ever stood near a helicopter when it's about to take off? Hold your hand near the bottom of the beater while someone is turning it. How much air movement do you feel?")

Eggbeater blades *circulate fluids.* They create voids in the beaten material and pull air into those voids. If the material being beaten is sticky, much of this air is trapped in the mass. Continued beating denatures the protein molecules in the egg white. ("What makes this foamy substance get stiff?") The molecules form a network and the once liquid mass no longer flows but holds its shape (see SEPARATION, page 30).

Make apple puffs to demonstrate the *leavening* effect of egg whites. When the students *fold in* the beaten egg whites, emphasize the need to be gentle so as not to burst the bubbles. ("Imagine tiny balloons in there.") Save a little of the *batter* to cook without adding egg whites; then compare the textures of the two batters when cooked.

Vocabulary

batter a flowing mass that is stirred or beaten, and that is used for making cakes, muffins, pancakes, and puffs

*blend to mix thoroughly

circulate to move from place to place

*diameter the length of a straight line through the center of a circle or a circular object

fluid a flowing substance, liquid or gas, that conforms to the shape of its container

fold in to blend ingredients gently, without stirring or beating; to mix slowly and gently by turning one ingredient over another

*griddle a heavy, flat metal pan used for cooking pancakes

leaven (verb) to make a batter rise; to lighten the consistency of a substance

Materials

eggbeater

peeler

grater

2 mixing bowls

measuring cups and spoons

griddle

oil to grease griddle

stove or hot plate

large spoon

ruler

spatula

fork and plate for each student

ingredients listed on experiment page

Discussion Questions

- What happens to the batter as it warms on the griddle? Why?

- What happens to the softness of the egg when it is cooked? Why? (See COAGULATION, page 18.) What happens if the egg is overcooked?

- What happens to the firmness of the apples when they are cooked? Why? (See SOFTENING, page 22.)

- How do egg whites affect the texture of the apple puffs?

Related Activities

- Compare Delicious, Stayman, York, and other varieties of apples for flavor and texture (mild, bitter, sour, tart, juicy, mealy, smooth, soft, crisp, and so on). Discuss the advantages of using tart, crisp apples rather than bland, soft ones in batter.

- Look at, feel, and smell a stick of cinnamon. The stick is made by peeling and then drying the inner bark from the branches of either the cinnamon or the cassia tree. Find out where these trees grow. (see SENSORY PERCEPTION, page 42).

- Investigate the source of nutmeg (see SENSORY PERCEPTION, page 42).

- Grate a nutmeg on a fine grater to release its odor. Use freshly grated nutmeg for making apple puffs.

Student worksheet, p. 75.

LEAVENING EXPERIMENT: WATCHING YEAST AND BAKING SODA IN ACTION

Yeast is a *single-celled* plant. It lies dormant when in a dry or frozen form, but nourishment and warm water enable it to grow and multiply. Honey and other sugars provide yeast with a quick supply of nourishment. The cells grow and reproduce best at 85-95°F. Their simple form of reproduction is called budding. ("It's as if from the skin of Jim grew a little Jim that broke off and made another, separate Jim.") Yeast cells give off *carbon dioxide* gas, just as we do when we breathe out.

Yeast mixtures are somewhat sticky and trap the carbon dioxide. Students can observe a slow, but impressive fermentation as the bubbly yeast mass rises to the top of its container and begins to overflow. This foaming, rising action is the basis of the leavening of most breads.

While waiting for the yeast to ferment in a warm place, go on to the *baking soda* experiment. (Do not confuse baking soda with baking powder, which is described on page 40, although both are *leavening* agents.) A molecule of sodium bicarbonate, or baking soda, is made up of the atoms of four elements—sodium, carbon, hydrogen, and oxygen. When an *acid* (such as vinegar) is added to baking soda, the atoms quickly recombine and carbon dioxide, a gas, is released. ("Why does the gas fizz from the water into the air? What happens when you push a ball to the bottom of a swimming pool?") This gas is lighter than water and rises to the top.

The chemical reaction is so fast that seeing it requires close attention. Build suspense and attentiveness by looking for a reaction with honey before looking for a reaction with vinegar.

Vocabulary

acid sour-tasting substance that combines with baking soda to release carbon dioxide

baking soda a substance which acts as a leaven when an acid is added to it

carbon dioxide a colorless gas produced when carbon combines with oxygen

fermentation the formation of gas bubbles as certain cells grow

leaven (noun) a substance that makes a batter lighter or less dense by producing a gas that pushes against the surrounding material; sometimes called leavening

single-celled made up of only one cell, such as bacteria and yeast

yeast a single-celled plant which grows and multiplies very quickly under certain conditions, and acts as a leavening agent

Materials

6 clear glasses or glass jars
6 labels
thermometer (good to above 100°F.)
measuring cup and spoons
ingredients listed on experiment page

Discussion Questions

• What is fermentation?
• How does yeast make carbon dioxide? Why is honey helpful? Why do the carbon dioxide bubbles rise to the top?
• How does baking soda make carbon dioxide? Why does the chemical reaction stop?
• Why does the yeast mixture take longer than soda and vinegar to make carbon dioxide?
• Would the yeast eventually stop making carbon dioxide unless you gave it more honey or other food? Why?
• Since yeast is living matter, what would happen to it if you boiled it? Froze it?
• Why would adding lemon to baking soda make it fizz?

Related Activities

• Dissolve baking soda in 2 cups warm water. Chill half and heat half of the solution. Pour vinegar into each solution and compare the rates of reaction.
• Apply the concept of geometric progression to the budding of a cell. ("How many Jims will there be if each Jim grows another Jim, and if all those Jims bud again?")
• Examine cells through a microscope or study photographs of cells.

• Make soda pop by adding ½ teaspoon baking soda to a glass of honey lemonade (see DISSOLUTION, page 5).

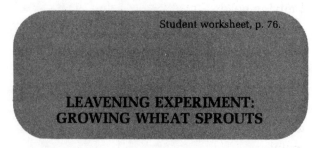

Student worksheet, p. 76.

LEAVENING EXPERIMENT: GROWING WHEAT SPROUTS

Along a dirt road bordering his wheat field, a grandfather walked with his ten-year-old granddaughter. "I'll show you how to make chewing gum," he said, while snapping a ripe head of grain from atop a brown wheat stalk. What he taught me (for I was the granddaughter), you can teach to your class to help them understand the leavening of bread. Just prepare ahead by pulling up some ripe wheat from the field of a friendly farmer at harvest time, or by ordering samples (see "Kernel of Wheat" in BIBLIOGRAPHY, page 50).

After snapping the head from a wheat stalk, rub it between your hands to loosen the husks, or *chaff*. ("I am *threshing* the wheat.") Now, gently blow the chaff from the palms of your hands, leaving the grain behind. ("I am *winnowing* the wheat. You try.")

With your front teeth, bite a grain in half to show the white starch inside the layers of bran. You will probably not be able to see the small germ in the grain. Now let each student bite a grain to look at it closely.

Finally, you are ready to make "chewing gum." Wheat contains a protein substance called *gluten*, which becomes elastic when chewed. Let the students crush and chew several grains of wheat for ten minutes. They will find that the wheat begins to stick together in their mouths, forming one mass. This experiment will demonstrate the elastic characteristic of wheat (and most other grains), which enables the batter or dough to stick together and trap the gas bubbles created by the leavening agent. *Kneading* dough develops its elasticity.

The *sprout* experiment demonstrates the potential within wheat grains to *germinate* into crops of wheat. Gluten is the protein substance used in the growth process, as the germ develops into root, stem, and leaves. When left in the sun or daylight, the tiny leaves of the sprouted wheat will begin to turn green, but note that they will become tough after more than a day of light.

Sprouts grown in a jar must be rinsed twice daily to prevent fungus from forming. They will keep for ten days if refrigerated after the last rinse. Be sure to use grains or seeds that have not been treated with chemicals.

Vocabulary

chaff the outer husk covering a kernel of grain

germinate to sprout, or start growing

gluten the protein substance in wheat flour which becomes sticky and elastic when moistened and stirred or kneaded

*invert to turn upside down

knead to work a mass of dough by pressing it with the palms of the hands so as to make the dough elastic

*mesh a net of woven threads or wires

sprout (noun) the young growth from the germ of a seed

thresh to separate the grain from the straw and chaff of the harvested grain plant by striking

winnow to blow away the chaff from the grain

Materials

wide-mouthed, clear glass jar

mesh (cheesecloth or a stocking)

rubber bands

measuring cup

ingredients listed on experiment page

Discussion Questions

• How is wheat similar to, and different from, grass?

• How are the stalks of wheat (straw) like the straws you drink though?

• In what ways can chaff be winnowed from grain?

• What property of wheat makes it similar to chewing gum?

• How is the germ of a wheat grain like the embryo of an egg? (see COAGULATION, page 18)

• What protein substance is supplied for use in the growth of a wheat sprout?

• Which parts of the new plant are beginning to show in the wheat sprout?

Related Activities

• Compare a stalk of wheat with grass gone to seed. Wheat was originally a wild grass, collected by early humans and improved over the ages by cultivation.

• Learn more about gluten, the elastic substance in wheat flour.

• Study a catalog of farm equipment to see how a combine harvests, threshes, and winnows grain.

• Find pictures of primitive ways of threshing and winnowing (see BIBLIOGRAPHY, page 47).

• Compare straw and hay as to their source and various uses.

• Learn about the protein in grains and how it complements the protein in nuts and beans to supply the essential amino acids needed for proper nutrition.

• Grow sprouts from alfalfa seeds, following the directions for growing wheat sprouts. The ideal length for alfalfa sprouts is one inch.

Student worksheet, p. 77.

LEAVENING EXPERIMENT: MAKING WHEAT GERM PANCAKES WITH BAKING POWDER

Baking powder is a sour-tasting mixture of baking soda and acid-producing ingredients that combine when moistened to release carbon dioxide. Because baking powder already contains an acid salt, you won't need to add vinegar to it to leaven pancakes. ("Taste a little baking powder. How does it taste?")

Single-acting baking powder reacts as soon as it becomes wet, so the batter needs to be used before the bubbles escape. Double-acting baking powder contains two acid salts: one reacts to moisture, and the other reacts to heat.

Have the students taste some wheat germ and discuss the flavor it will add to the pancakes.

("Why should we use wheat germ and whole wheat flour?") The germ is the embryo of the wheat grain. Point out that the germ has more minerals, vitamins, and protein than an equal amount of whole wheat or white flour. The latter has the least nutrients and the least flavor. Discuss the difference between whole wheat and white flour.

Review fractions by having students divide the recipe given in half. ("Half of this recipe is enough for 12 pancakes. How do we figure out half of a recipe?") Use apple sections, drawings, money (quarters), and Cuisenaire rods to discover ½ of 1½. If the students understand that 3 teaspoons make 1 tablespoon, they may reason that they can measure 1 teaspoon plus ½ teaspoon of honey to make ½ tablespoon of honey. To allow time for thinking these ideas through, you might make this a separate lesson.

Toss a few drops of water on to the griddle as it heats. ("What is happening to the water?") Let it evaporate before tossing on more drops. When the heat produces a bubbly dancing of the drops, the griddle is ready for cooking pancakes.

Be sure to observe the pancakes as they expand on the griddle. Discuss what is happening. Restrain the temptation to press down on the pancakes with the spatula.

Don't mask the flavor of the pancakes by using syrup. ("What ingredients can you taste?") Break open a pancake to see the spaces made by the carbon dioxide inside.

Vocabulary

baking powder a mixture of baking soda and acid-producing substances that combine when wet to release carbon dioxide and act as a leavening agent

Materials

measuring cups and spoons

mixing spoon

2 mixing bowls—1 small, 1 large

eggbeater

griddle

oil to grease griddle

spatula

stove or hot plate

fork and plate for each student

ingredients listed on experiment page

Discussion Questions

- Why do you need to blend the ingredients?
- Why shouldn't you press down on the pancakes as they cook?
- Why don't you taste the sour baking powder after the pancakes have risen?
- Why is a griddle better than a skillet for making pancakes?
- Which is larger—¼ or ½; ¾ or ½; ¾ or 1?

Related Activities

- In a quiet place, experiment with single-acting and double-acting baking powders in separate glasses. First add cool water and stir. Listen until the action stops. Compare the results in the two glasses. Then pour in boiling water. Look, listen, and compare.
- Estimate what fraction of a mixing spoon a tablespoon of batter fills. Estimate the capacity of the mixing spoon in terms of tablespoons. Check your estimates with a measuring spoon.

Student worksheet, p. 78.

LEAVENING EXPERIMENT: MAKING WHEAT GERM PANCAKES WITH YEAST

Yeast cells feed on honey as they grow (see Watching Yeast and Baking Soda in Action, page 37). In addition, they produce enzymes which slowly turn starch into sugar to further nourish yeast growth. Thus, both honey (or any other sugar) and wheat starch contribute to the development of yeast cells in *dough*.

Yeast breads should have time to rise slowly if the dough is to be tender and filled with small bubbles. A long rising time doesn't seem as critical with pancake batter, but, as with bread dough, all ingredients should be between 80°–90°F. so that the yeast will begin to ferment right away.

Fermentation produces alcohol as well as carbon dioxide, imparting the characteristic smell of a brewery to dough. Baking evaporates the alcohol and kills the yeast cells, but much of the yeast-produced flavor remains.

Commercial yeast is a standardized product, but wild yeast *spores* float in the air everywhere and will breed within a week if trapped and kept warm in a combination of flour, honey, and milk or water. This mixture can then be used to leaven dough. It has a sour taste because of the acid produced during the long period of fermentation. When baked, the result is known as *sourdough* bread.

The nutritive value and flavor of yeast breads differs from that of baking powder products. This is because wheat is a rich source of B vitamins, and the baking soda in baking powder destroys a significant portion of these.

As you watch the pancakes rise on the griddle, discuss the cause of the action. When you eat the pancakes, talk about their flavor and texture and compare them with the flavor and texture of the baking powder pancakes.

Vocabulary

dough a mixture of flour and other ingredients, often leavened with yeast, forming a thick mass that can be worked by hand for making bread and other baked goods

sourdough a bread made by trapping natural yeast spores found in the air

spore a tiny single-celled body capable of developing into a living cell

Materials

measuring cups and spoons

mixing spoon

2 mixing bowls—1 small, 1 large

eggbeater

griddle

oil to grease griddle

spatula

stove or hot plate

fork and plate for each student

ingredients listed on experiment page

Discussion Questions

- How do yeast and baking powder compare with egg whites in the way they leaven batter?
- Aside from flavor, what is the reason for using some form of sugar (such as honey) in yeast batters?
- Why did we use honey in the baking powder pancakes?
- Why should the ingredients for a yeast dough be warm?
- How would too high a temperature affect the yeast?
- Why do the yeast and baking powder pancakes taste different? Why alike?
- Why don't the recipes for cakes and other delicately flavored baked goods call for yeast?
- Why does a yeast mixture smell like beer?

Related Activities

- Locate a recipe for yeast muffins and make them.
- Visit a bakery and learn about the leavenings used by its bakers.
- Learn about breads from other parts of the world, such as tortillas and matzos, which are both unleavened. (The history of matzos is fascinating.)
- Compare recipes in other cookbooks to see which use yeast and which use baking powder.
- Learn about the difference between baker's yeast and brewer's yeast.

9

Sensory Perception: How Do Herbs and Spices Flavor Our Food?

Touch! Feel! Squeeze! Smell! This is how to approach seasonings. ("Do you have a spice shelf at home? What is on it?") Examine and discuss herbs and spices. ("What food would taste good with this added? How much would you use?")

Spice is often used in a general way to mean any seasoning for food. Specifically contrasted with herb, spice usually indicates the product of a tropical plant—its root, bark, flower, fruit, or seed. Herb refers to the leaves, and sometimes to the seeds, of a plant usually grown in temperate climates.

Herbs and spices should be used sparingly to enhance the flavor of foods, and to make a dish smell and taste appetizing, not to overpower the food with the strong flavor of the seasoning. They should be used to stimulate the appetite and the digestive juices, not to bombard the senses.

Encourage students to taste small pieces of bitter chocolate, drops of vanilla, drops of lemon juice, a few grains of salt, and a few grains of sugar. Which areas of the tongue are most sensitive to each of these substances? Students should hold their noses so that they don't confuse taste with smell. With eyes closed and relying on taste alone, the students can try to identify an herb or a spice, or distinguish between lemon and grapefruit juice. It's difficult. When noses are let go, the task is easier. It should be evident that our sense of smell works with our sense of taste when we eat. This is because the volatile molecules from the food first circulate in the air and then travel up to the olfactory sensors in our noses, so we "taste" the flavor with our noses!

Objectives

- To relate information about nerves to the senses of smell and taste
- To familiarize students with the qualities and uses of herbs and spices
- To teach geographical locations and climates in connection with sources of herbs and spices

Applied Skills

Motor Skills: drawing herb plants from observation, crushing dried herbs, grating, whisking, cutting chives with scissors, stirring, blending with a fork, adding ingredients slowly

Measuring: measuring weight, length, volume

Observing: noting differences in fresh and dried herbs, comparing flavors of herbs, observing flavors of spices

Coordinating Movements: one person beating while another adds ingredients

Key Ideas

- Nerves carry messages to and from the brain.
- The brain is made aware of food flavors by the nerve sensors of taste and smell.

42

- The nerve cells for taste are connected to taste buds on the tongue.
- Taste buds are receptive to only four basic tastes: sweet, salt, sour, and bitter.
- The olfactory nerve cells are connected to nerve endings in the nasal cavity which are sensitive to volatile substances.
- A pound contains 16 ounces.

SENSORY PERCEPTION EXPERIMENT: IDENTIFYING HERBS

Student worksheet, p. 79.

This lesson on identifying *herbs* was first inspired on a dreary winter day after Christmas. Crunching my way through dirty snow, I reached a greenhouse that was void of customers but replete with energetic young herb plants—savory, thyme, oregano, marjoram, parsley, basil, rosemary, sage—responding to the lengthening days. While savoring the environment, I selected eight plants for variety of use and appearance.

When you visit an herb greenhouse, or take samples from an herb garden, don't feel limited by the experiment's list of herbs. Choose a variety of herbs that appeal to you. If you wish, get the same herbs in dried form to compare with the living plants.

Taste buds cannot discriminate between the flavors of various herbs. Located in little wells between the bumps on the tongue and in distinct areas on the tongue, these *nerve* cells respond to one of only four tastes: sweetness is usually sensed on the tip of the tongue, sourness on the sides, saltiness on both the sides and the tip, and bitterness at the back.

The *olfactory sense organ*, on the other hand, is able to discriminate between hundreds of odors. Located in the mucous membrane in the upper part of the *nasal cavity*, these nerve cells are sensitive to substances in gaseous form. Squeeze an herb. ("How does the smell reach your nose?") The *volatile* molecules of the herb are transmitted through the air to the nasal cavity. At a meal, you detect smells emitted from the food on your plate, or as you lift it to your mouth. Then as part of the tasting process, you detect the smells from inside your mouth as the molecules travel by way of the throat to the nasal cavity.

Vocabulary

herb a plant whose leaves are used for seasonings and which is usually grown in temperate climates

nasal cavity the space in the head behind the nostrils through which air passes to the throat on its way to the lungs

nerve a single cell, or a structure made up of cells, that carries messages from one part of the body to another

olfactory related to the sense of smell

sense organ a bodily structure, such as the nose, which receives a stimulus, such as the odor of an herb, and responds by sending messages to the brain where they are interpreted as sensations

volatile evaporating quickly, moving about quickly

Materials

drawing paper

pencils

herbs listed on experiment page

Discussion Questions

- What four flavors can your tongue taste?
- How do smells contribute to the flavor of foods?
- What are herbs?
- Why are herbs used?
- Why is your nasal cavity an appropriate location for the olfactory sense organ?
- What flavors could you taste if you had a stuffy head cold? What flavors would the cold keep you from enjoying?

Related Activities

- Plant herb seeds to start your own herb garden.
- Learn how to dry herbs (see EVAPORATION, page 12).
- Read an herb chart to find foods which can be enhanced by the herbs you have studied.
- Learn the food value of parsley.

- Buy mint or other herb tea and brew some.
- Crush fresh mint and add to honey lemonade (see DISSOLUTION, page 5).
- Discuss the herb-like quality of celery leaves in the creamed celery recipe (see Making Creamed Celery, page 29).

Student worksheet, p. 80.

SENSORY PERCEPTION EXPERIMENT: MAKING CHEESE TOM DITTY

When I was young, before the days of pizza's popularity, my mother often made a lunch dish called "Rub Tum Ditty" on winter weekends. Irma Rombauer, in *The Joy of Cooking* (1946 edition), calls a similar recipe "Rink Tum Diddy Rarebit." "Cheese Tom Ditty" seems more descriptive, and "Tomato Rarebit" would also be fitting. A ditty is a short, simple song, and this recipe makes a quick and simple dish. The name "Rarebit" (pronounced "rer-bit") is derived from "Welsh Rabbit," a humorous name for a melted-cheese mixture served on toast or crackers. Students who make this dish often remember it simply as "that pizza rather than Cheese Tom Ditty."

Oregano, the strong herb associated with pizza, is used to flavor Cheese Tom Ditty. Oregano is a major ingredient of chili powder and also is a good seasoning for pork or chicken. Grown from the tiniest of seeds, oregano has oval gray-green leaves and small, fuzzy white blossoms.

Ask students to smell the oregano repeatedly. They may discover that they can no longer detect the *aroma*. This is because the olfactory nerve becomes fatigued, to the extent of being *desensitized*, by continued exposure to a particular odor. The nerve remains alert for other odors, but each new odor, in turn, fatigues the nerve. Thus you get used to particular smells until the nerves are given a rest from them for a while.

Vocabulary

aroma fragrance, pleasant odor

desensitized not able to be excited or affected any longer by a specific substance or event

oregano an herb plant belonging to the mint family whose leaves have a strong, warm, and pleasantly bitter flavor

Materials

small saucepan

wire whisk

oven or toaster

stove or hot plate

measuring cups and spoons

grater

knife to cut bread

serving spoon

fork and spoon for each student

ingredients listed on experiment page

Discussion Questions

- What ingredients make Cheese Tom Ditty taste like pizza?
- How does Cheese Tom Ditty differ from pizza?
- How does your brain get the message of an herb's flavor?
- What happens when you smell an herb for a long time? Why?

Related Activities

- Compare the subtle differences in flavor and appearance of oregano, marjoram, and savory. Find recipes using these herbs.
- Classify herbs by their predominately bitter or sweet flavor.
- Investigate the ways in which the sense of touch influences flavor; consider, for example, crunchy celery, smooth pudding, and so on.
- Discuss the aroma of such foods as onions, roast meats, and strawberries, all of which can be detected at some distance.
- Learn about artificial flavorings, which are manufactured from chemicals.

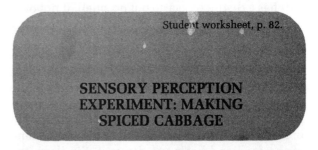

Student worksheet, p. 81.

SENSORY PERCEPTION EXPERIMENT: MAKING CELERY LOGS WITH CHIVES

Daffodils and onions are easily grown by planting their *bulbs*. ("How are potatoes started? Where do the sprouts get their first nourishment? How are bulbs similar to sprouting potatoes? How are they different?" [see Twice-Baked Potatoes, page 24]).

Bulb plants reproduce by three methods: bulbs multiply undergound, seeds form within blooms, and/or miniature bulbs develop within blooms. *Propagation* of the underground bulbs is the easiest method for growing new *chives* plants.

Cut open an onion and look for the embryonic plant in the center. It is surrounded and nourished by fleshy, thick, white layers. Chives, which resemble miniature onions, also grow from bulbs. Their soft, tubular, bright green leaves seem to erupt straight from the dirt. In spring, stiff, tubular stalks appear among the chive leaves. These stalks bear flowers—fluffy, lavender balls.

The chive leaves (hence it is an herb) are chopped and used to impart a mild onion flavor to foods. The chopping can be accomplished easily with scissors.

Check the weight of the cream cheese on a scale. Calculate how many 3-ounce packages it would take to make 1 pound of cream cheese. Cut a package into thirds. ("How much does one section weigh? How heavy does 1 ounce feel?")

Vocabulary

bulb a storage unit and embryonic plant which usually begins to grow undergound (the roots pushing out from its base, the stem and leaves emerging from the top)

chives herb plants that grow from a bulb and have leaves with a mild onion-like flavor

propagation the process whereby a plant or animal reproduces

Materials

small bowl

3 or more knives

several forks

scissors

ruler

cutting board

measuring spoons

serving plate

ingredients listed on experiment page

Discussion Questions

- How is a bulb different from a potato tuber?
- What part covers a bulb and helps keep it fresh after it has been taken out of the ground?
- How do chives propagate?
- Which part of the chives plant is usually used for seasoning?
- What do chives taste like?
- How many 3-ounce packages of cream cheese would you need to make 1 pound? How many 8-oz. packages would you need?

Related Activities

- Buy a small cluster of chives and plant it in rich garden soil in the spring.
- Separate a bulb of garlic into cloves. Compare this bulb with onion and chives bulbs. Plant the cloves in the spring.
- Plant flower bulbs outdoors in the fall. Dig them up after they bloom in the spring to see if the bulb has generated little bulbs.
- Grow white narcissus indoors from bulbs.
- Add chopped chives to omelets, salads, or baked potatoes.

Student worksheet, p. 82.

SENSORY PERCEPTION EXPERIMENT: MAKING SPICED CABBAGE

Cloves are dried buds of a flower from tropical trees that grow 15 to 30 feet tall. The word "clove" comes from the French word for "nail." ("What does a clove look like to you?") Do not confuse cloves, the *spice*, with the cloves, or sections, of a garlic bulb. Whole cloves are used to flavor and decorate hams. Finely ground they are used in gingerbread. The powder is too *pungent* to be used in spiced cabbage, but a few "nails" always lend a pleasant flavor to any cooked cabbage.

Nutmeg and cinnamon (see Making Apple Puffs, page 36), also grow in the tropics. The large nutmeg tree bears a pear-shaped fruit whose seed is what we know as whole nutmeg. Grating the meat of this pungent, brown-flecked seed is a pleasant experience. Cinnamon comes from the bark peeled from the cinnamon or cassia tree, both of the laurel family. Cassia bark has a stronger flavor and is preferred in this country. The dried and tightly curled sticks of this bark are usually ground commercially.

The flavor of the spice called *allspice* resembles a blend of cloves, nutmeg, and cinnamon. Allspice is the unripe berry of the pimento tree, which grows only in the Western Hemisphere.

Black pepper comes from vinelike pepper plants which are trained to climb up tall poles. The red berries of this vine turn black when they are dried. The berries, called peppercorns, are ground to make the most popular spice in the world. White pepper is made from the lighter, inner part of the peppercorn.

Paprika comes from the fruit of another kind of pepper plant. The dried pod of this plant is powdered to make the warm-flavored, coppery-red spice used on deviled eggs (see Making Deviled Eggs, page 20).

Vanilla is extracted from the seed pod of an orchid plant. It enhances many desserts and flavors whipped cream (see Making Whipped Cream, page 33).

Salt belongs in a category by itself. Mined from the ground, or collected by evaporating sea water, it is a mineral rather than a plant substance. Salt has a distinctive taste but no smell. It not only enhances the flavors of foods, but it also has many chemical uses and is essential to life itself.

Our bodies react to spices in a complicated manner. Olfactory nerve cells, located in the nose, receive spice molecules and send messages to the brain through the olfactory nerve. The brain responds by sending a message to the tongue to increase the flow of saliva. Saliva dissolves some of the food and begins to digest it. Similarly, the brain stimulates other digestive juices throughout the digestive system. Along with pleasant colors and textures, which appeal to the senses of sight and touch, pleasant aromas stimulate the appetite.

In the spiced cabbage experiment there are many complementary flavors to stimulate the brain: sweet, sour, salty, and bitter—plus the aroma of spices.

Vocabulary

allspice a spice produced by drying the unripe berry of a tropical pimento tree

cloves a spice produced by drying the bud of a flower which grows on a tropical tree

pungent sharp and stinging to the taste

spice the product of a tropical plant's roots, bark, flower, fruit, or seeds; used for seasoning

Materials

grater with varied hole sizes

measuring cups and spoons

large skillet with lid

mixing spoon

stove or hot plate

fork and plate for each student

ingredients listed on experiment page

Discussion Questions

- What flavors can your senses detect in the spiced cabbage?
- What are spices?
- Why should foods have pleasant smells and flavors?
- How does the cooking process affect the cellulose in cabbage?

Related Activities

- Make a clove ball by inserting cloves in an orange until it is completely covered with them. The cloves will preserve the orange.
- On the globe, locate the areas where spices are grown.
- Study the history of the use of spices to preserve foods. Read about the voyages of Marco Polo. Learn how the need for spices led to the explorations of Columbus.
- Investigate the sense of touch on the tongue. Discuss the ways in which texture and temperature affect the enjoyment of food.

Bibliography

The numbers in parentheses denote the units that these sources supplement. "G" denotes cookbooks or books with general application.

Books

ABERCROMBIE, THOMAS J. "Egypt," *National Geographic*, March 1977, p. 341. This picture of wheat being winnowed evokes interest after students have winnowed grain in the palms of their hands. (8)

ALLARD, WILLIAM ALBERT. "Chief Joseph," *National Geographic*, March 1977, pp. 424–25. A color photograph of a huge, partially cut wheat field in Washington State, including a combine. (8)

BARON, HENRIETTA. *Breakfast*. Everybody Can Cook, vol. 1 (Seattle, Wash.: Special Child Publications, 1977). Illustrates rules for shopping, table setting, washing dishes, and preparing the simplest fruit juice. Also includes more complex recipes, such as for buckwheat cakes. Each detail is clearly illustrated, point by point. (G)

BECK, BARBARA L. *The First Book of Fruits* (New York: Franklin Watts, 1967). Fruits are defined, botanically described, classified, and beautifully depicted. Some leaves, trees, and cross sections are illustrated. Each fruit's origin, use, and geographical location are provided, along with an interesting fact or two. (2,3,8)

BECK, BARBARA L. *Vegetables* (New York: Franklin Watts, 1970). Grouped in families, both common and exotic vegetables are beautifully illustrated by Page Cary. The history, growth, and uses of vegetables are covered succinctly. (2, 3, 5, 6, 9)

BRUNO, JANET, AND PEGGY DAKAN. *Cooking in the Classroom* (Belmont, Ca.: Fearon Pitman Publishers, Inc., 1974). Very simple, amusingly illustrated recipes, accompanied by word lists. Questions call for use of the senses. Many recipes do not require a stove. (G)

BUCHHEIMER, NAOMI. *Let's Go to a Bakery* (New York: G. P. Putnam's Sons, 1956). An instructive book for those who have made bread on a small scale. It should probably be complemented by a field trip. (8)

COBB, VICKI. *Science Experiments You Can Eat* (New York and Philadelphia: J. B. Lippincott, 1972). Solutions, suspensions, cellulose, and oxidation are just some of the many ideas to explore in this book. A parent or teacher can apply them at any level; upper elementary and junior high students should be able to experiment on their own. (1, 2, 4, 5, 7, 8)

COLLINS, MARY. *Spices of the World Cookbook by McCormick* (New York: Penguin Books, 1969). Complete and informative, this cookbook includes the history and source of each herb and spice and a supplementary index listing the recipes in which each spice is used. (3, 4, 7, 8, 9)

COOPER, ELIZABETH K. *And Everything Nice* (New York: Harcourt, Brace and World, 1966). Explores the history and uses of cinnamon, cloves, nutmeg, pepper, paprika, vanilla, and other seasonings. Some of the line drawings by Julie Maas are graphic and imaginative. (4, 7, 8, 9)

COSGROVE, MARGARET. *Eggs—And What Happens Inside Them* (New York: Dodd, Mead, 1966). Cell development of humans, fish, reptiles, birds, kangaroos, and other animals is described and illustrated. (4)

CROCKER, BETTY. *Betty Crocker's Cookbook for Boys and Girls* (New York: Golden Press, 1975). Appealing recipes are accompanied by beautiful photographs. The step-by-step directions follow a clear presentation of utensils and ingredients needed. (G)

DALY, KATHLEEN N. "The Wonderful Egg," Ranger Rick, July 1976, pp. 41–43. Several photographs, including a cutaway egg containing a developing chicken, and a broken egg with a wet chicken ready to emerge, accompany a text which describes the evolution of bird eggs from fish eggs and amphibian eggs. (4)

DAVIS, ADELE. *Let's Cook It Right* (New York: Harcourt Brace Jovanovich, 1970). A complete cookbook that provides healthful recipes as well as detailed explanations of how to cook to save nutrients. (G)

DAVIS, BARBARA. *Learning Science and Metric Through Cooking* (New York: Sterling Publishing, 1964). Good for content, but not organized for teaching, this book combines experiments and recipes. It is directed to the child and could be a springboard for months of concept development. (4, 7, 8, 9)

EBERLE, IRMENGARDE. *Basketful, the Story of Our Foods* (New York: Thomas Y. Crowell, 1946). Apples, honey, and wheat are a few of the foods discussed. (1, 3, 6, 8)

EBERLE, IRMENGARDE. *Grasses* (New York: Henry Z. Walck, 1960). Brief, illustrated accounts of wheat, hay, rice, corn, sugar cane and bamboo provide interesting variety. (6, 7, 8)

FABER, DORIS. *The Miracle of Vitamins* (New York: G. P. Putnam's Sons, 1964). Suspenseful stories relate the discoveries of many vitamins. The book conveys the importance of nutrition and also discusses diet fads. (4, 5, 8)

FENTON, CARROLL LANE, AND HERMINIE B. KITCHEN. *Fruits We Eat* (New York: John Day, 1961). The histories of, as well as legends about, common and exotic fruits, classified by family. The 150 drawings by Carroll Lane Fenton are exquisite. (2, 3, 8)

FLANAGAN, GERALDINE LUX. *Window Into an Egg. Seeing Life Begin* (New York: Young Scott Books, 1969). Superb photographs of the chick as it develops inside the shell

complement a simplified and helpfully analogized description of the process. (4, 7)

FOSTER, VIRGIL E. *Close-Up of a Honeybee* (New York: Young Scott Books, 1960). Foster's photographs of bees and bee-keeping accompany narratives about experiences with bees. Honey-making and bee stings are explained. (1)

FREEMAN, MAE, AND IRA FREEMAN. *The Story of Chemistry* (New York: Random House, 1962). The structure of matter and the nature of chemical changes are explained at an elementary reading level. (1, 3, 6)

GORAN, MORRIS. *Experimental Chemistry for Boys* (New York: John F. Rider Publisher, 1961). Lab procedures and science theories are applied to everyday substances. Defines suspensions, colloids, solutions, atoms, molecules, and compounds. Organic chemistry is applied to cooking, and experiments with oxidation are described. (1, 2, 3, 7)

HAMMOND, WINIFRED G. *Plants, Food, and People* (New York: Coward-McCann, 1964). Farming techniques are explained beginning with early hunting and gathering, and continuing through the use of modern threshing machines. (6, 8)

HANDEL, RUTH D., AND MARVIN SPIEGELMAN. *The Reader in the Kitchen* (Ridgefield, N.J.: Educational Performance Association, 1976). Oriented towards developing the skills of listening, looking, speaking, word recognition, and comprehension. The authors take the child to the market, introduce food games, and present 21 recipes in order of increasing difficulty. (G)

HERTZBERG, RUTH, BEATRICE VAUGHAN, AND JANET GREENE. *Putting Food By* (Brattleboro, Vt.: Stephen Greene Press, 1973). A comprehensive text about the techniques of preserving foods. Includes 50 pages about drying foods. (2, 3)

McCLENAHAN, PAT, AND IDA JAQUA. *Cool Cooking for Kids* (Belmont, Ca.: Fearon Pitman Publishers, Inc., 1976). 162 pages of interesting and useful ideas for teaching students of any age. The students develop language and concepts while they dissect fish, incubate eggs, or make pizza. (G)

MEYER, LILLIAN HOAGLAND. *Food Chemistry* (New York: Reinhold Publishing, 1960). A college text on the composition of foods and the changes that occur in processing. A helpful and interesting reference containing detailed and varied studies that have been done on foods. (G)

ROMBAUER, IRMA S. *The Joy of Cooking* (Indianapolis: Bobbs-Merrill, 1946). An old standby, this is a complete cookbook with explicit directions, helpful explanations, and interesting anecdotes. (G)

ROMBAUER, IRMA S., AND MARION ROMBAUER BECKER. *Joy of Cooking* (Indianapolis: Bobbs-Merrill, 1964). Now a classic, revised and expanded. Some favorite recipes from the old edition are not included. (G)

SELSAM, MILLICENT E. *The Carrot and Other Root Vegetables* (New York: William Morrow, 1971). Detailed photographs help explain the reproduction and development of root vegetables. (5)

SELSAM, MILLICENT E. *Play with Plants* (New York: William Morrow, 1949). How to grow plants from root vegetables, stems, and leaves and how to do experiments with seeds and plants. (5, 8)

SELSAM, MILLICENT E. *Tomatoes and Other Fruit Vegetables* (New York: William Morrow, 1970). Superb photographs which make use of color, cross sections, and macrophotography. (3, 5)

SELSAM, MILLICENT, AND DEBORAH PETERSON. *The Don't Throw It, Grow It Book of Houseplants* (New York: Random House, 1977). After we've eaten the fruit, so many seeds are thrown away! The authors give careful instructions for planting the seeds instead. Directions for raising the plants and drawings of what to expect make this a practical and inspiring book. (5)

SIMON, SEYMOUR. *Projects with Plants* (New York: Franklin Watts, 1973). Experiments with germination, nourishment, photosynthesis, molding, and many other aspects of plant growth are presented with clear directions. (3, 5, 6, 8)

STONE, A. HARRIS. *The Chemistry of a Lemon* (Englewood Cliffs, N.J.: Prentice-Hall, 1966). The many questions that follow the simple experiments with lemons deal with the ways lemons can make foam, coagulate protein, dissolve oxides, and change the colors of substances. (1, 2, 4, 8)

STRAUSS, JACQUELINE HARRIS. *Let's Experiment* (New York: Harper & Row, 1962). Requiring few materials, these safe, fun experiments are readable at a middle elementary level. They include testing for acid with cabbage and experimenting with the effects of acid on milk. Simple explanations are offered. (4, 6, 8, 9)

WEISS, MALCOLM E., AND ANN E. WEISS. *The Vitamin Puzzle* (New York: Simon & Schuster, 1976). The illustrations by Pat De Aloe complement an energetic presentation of the discoveries of, and need for, specific vitamins. Problems caused by too many vitamins, by the FDA, and by advertisers are also discussed. (4, 5, 8)

Young Children's Mix and Fix Cookbook (New York: Parents' Magazine Enterprises, 1975). Illustrated with cartoons on every page, the simple recipes are introduced with a motivating sentence and are clearly explained. Recipes need to be read in advance to determine equipment and materials needed. (G)

YOUNG, GORDON. "Salt—The Essence of Life," *National Geographic*, September 1977, pp. 380–401. The sources, history, structure, and chemistry of salt are described and illustrated. (9)

ZIM, HERBERT S. *What's Inside of Plants?* (New York: William S. Morrow, 1952). Botany for all ages in 32 pages, containing explicit color drawings of the inner structure and workings of roots, stems, leaves, flowers, fruits, and seeds. (5)

ZIM, HERBERT S. *Your Food and You* (New York: William Morrow, 1957). This book explains how the body breaks down and uses proteins, carbohydrates, and fats, and the functions and uses of minerals and vitamins. Likes and dislikes, allergies, and food poisoning are also discussed. Explicit tables and diagrams by Gustav Schrotter add interest to every page. (3, 4, 5, 6, 8)

Most topics covered in *The Science Cookbook* are clearly described in *The World Book Encyclopedia*. The McGraw-Hill *Encyclopedia of Science and Technology* is also a helpful reference.

Pamphlets, Posters, and Samples

"COOKING IS FUN," National Dairy Council, Chicago, Ill. 60606, 1972. A fifteen page pamphlet of simple recipes for the young, beginning cook. The supplies needed are presented in illustrations. (G)

"How Your Body Uses Food," by Albert Piltz, National Dairy Council, Rosemont, Ill. 60018, 1976. Twenty-six pages explain and diagram the way the body puts proteins, carbohydrates, fats, minerals, and vitamins to use. (4, 5, 6, 8)

"Kernel of Wheat," Kansas Wheat Commission, 1021 N. Main St., Hutchinson, Kan. 67501. A 16×22 in. poster of a cutaway wheat grain enlarged 70 times. It also comes in an 8½×11 in. size. A postcard picturing wheat growing is available, too. Attached to the card is a plastic pouch containing a few grains inside a head of wheat. (8)

"The Story of Wheat," Great Plains Wheat, Inc., Suite 340, 1030 15th St. NW, Washington, D.C. An eight-page pamphlet on the history and geography of wheat and the milling of flour. (8)

"The World of Wheat," Oregon Wheat Commission, 305 SW 10th, P.O. Box 400, Pendleton, Ore. 97801. Included are locations for wheat growing, kinds of flour and their uses, the nutrients in wheat, the reasons for using each specific cake ingredient, and a step-by-step explanation of how to make bread. (8)

Catalogs of Combines: Call farm machinery dealers listed in the yellow pages for catalogs. Some include diagrams of the harvesting/threshing process. (8)

Index of Vocabulary Words

51

Experiment Pages (Duplicatable)

Dissolution Experiment:
Making a Solution

Ingredients

6 teaspoons honey
water
ice

Directions

1. Measure 2 teaspoons honey (the solute) into each of 3 glasses.
2. Label the glasses "boiling," "room temperature," and "cold."
3. Prepare these solvents. Keep a thermometer in each and watch it.
   a. 1 cup boiling water
   b. 1 cup room temperature water
   c. 1 cup cold water

4. Pour the solvents slowly, all at the same time, into the right glasses.
5. Don't stir. Which solvent dissolves the honey first? Next? Last?
6. See if the honey has diffused. You can do this by tasting some of the liquid from the top of the glass. Gently dip it out with a spoon. Don't stir it.
7. Save the solutions for "Making Honey Lemonade."

Dissolution Experiment:
Making Honey Lemonade

Ingredients

Amounts for 1 person:
2 tablespoons lemon juice
2 teaspoons honey
1 cup water (warm or cold, but not boiling)
ice to fill each glass

Amounts for 3 persons, using the solutions you already made:
6 tablespoons lemon juice
3 cups of solutions already made

For more than 3 persons, using the solutions already made, put the number of persons in the first blank in each problem:
(____ × 2) = _____ tablespoons lemon juice
(____ × 2) − 6 = _____ teaspoons honey
(____ × 2) − 3 = _____ cups water
3 cups of solutions already made

Directions

1. Squeeze the lemon juice and take out the seeds.
2. Measure the juice and pour it into a pitcher.
3. Add honey and water.
4. Stir the mixture to dissolve the honey.
5. If you are preparing lemonade for 3 or more persons, add the solutions left from the experiment "Making a Solution." Stir.
6. Pour the mixture over ice in each glass.

Oxidation Experiment:
Watching Air Discolor Fresh Fruit

Ingredients

1 lemon

1 apple, 1 pear, 1 peach, some berries and any other fruits

meringue shells, whipped cream (optional)

Directions

1. Set out 3 dishes. Label them "lemon juice," "water," and "control."
2. Squeeze the lemon. Pour the juice into a small bowl.
3. Pour ¼ cup cold water into another small bowl.
4. Peel and slice an apple.
5. Dip ⅓ of the apple slices in lemon juice. Spread them out in the dish with the "lemon juice" label.
6. Dip ⅓ of the apple slices in water. Spread them out in the dish with the "water" label.
7. Put the rest of the apple slices in the dish labeled "control."
8. Repeat steps 4–7 with the other fruits.
9. Look at the fruits in each dish after 30 minutes. Compare what has happened to the fruits in each dish. The change you see is oxidation.
10. Mix the fruits and serve them in bowls. Or, cut them into small pieces and scoop them into meringue shells and top them with whipped cream.

Oxidation Experiment:
Making Slim-Slice Potato Cake

Ingredients

3 medium potatoes
1 teaspoon onion powder
½ teaspoon salt
dash of pepper
2 tablespoons salad oil or butter

Directions

1. Wash the potatoes. Take out the eyes. For maximum nutrition and flavor, do not peel the potatoes.
2. Make very thin slices of potato using a potato peeler.
3. Sprinkle salt and pepper onto the potato slices.
4. Heat oil in the skillet over medium heat.
5. Spread the potato slices evenly in the pan. Press them down with a spatula.
6. Cover the pan with a lid.
7. After 5 minutes, gently lift one edge of the potato cake. When it looks golden brown underneath, roll the cake over with two spatulas. Brown the cake on the other side.
8. Cut into wedges and serve.

Evaporation Experiment:
Evaporating Water

EVAPORATION AND HEAT

Directions

1. Measure 1 tablespoon water into each of 2 metal pie pans.
2. Record the time in Table 1.
3. Boil the water in one pan. Leave the water in the other pan at room temperature.
4. Record in Table 1 the time when the last drop of water evaporates from each pan.
5. Compare the evaporating times.

EVAPORATION AND AIR CIRCULATION

Directions

1. Make 2 wet streaks on a chalkboard with a sponge. Make the first streak as far as possible from the second one.
2. Record the time in Table 1.
3. Fan one streak with a newspaper, cookie sheet, or fan. Leave the other streak alone.
4. Record in Table 1 the time when the last drop of water evaporates from each streak.
5. Compare the drying times.

Table 1. Speed of Evaporation of Water

	EVAPORATION OF TABLESPOON OF WATER		EVAPORATION OF WET STREAK	
	Room temperature	Boiling	Left alone	Fanned
Time evaporation was begun				
Time evaporation was complete				
Time required for evaporation				
Time comparisons	Room temperature _____ minutes Boiling _____ minutes = _____ times longer		Left alone _____ minutes Fanned _____ minutes = _____ times longer	

Example: Room temperature __130__ minutes; Boiling __2__ minutes, = __65__ times longer.

Evaporation Experiment:
Making Stewed Tomatoes

Ingredients

1 16-ounce can tomatoes
1 garlic clove, peeled and mashed with the broad blade of a knife
1 medium onion, chopped
1 stalk celery with leaves, sliced (optional)
¼ teaspoon salt
½ teaspoon dried oregano
1 teaspoon brown sugar

Directions

1. Put the can of tomatoes and their juice into a frying pan. Chop up large pieces with the edge of a spoon.
2. Bring to a boil over medium heat.
3. Add mashed garlic and chopped onion. Add celery (optional). Cover.
4. Simmer over low heat for 10 minutes.
5. Uncover. Add the remaining ingredients.
6. Simmer, uncovered, until the juice has evaporated (about 10 minutes). Stir now and then to prevent sticking.
7. Spoon onto plates and serve.

Evaporation Experiment:
Drying Apples

Ingredients

2 firm apples, preferably tart
antioxidant (optional):
  juice of 1 lemon, or
  1,000 mg. vitamin C pills, dissolved in
    2 tablespoons water, or
  ascorbic acid, pure or mixed, made according to directions on the bttle

Directions

1. Preheat oven to 150°F.
2. Core and peel the apples.
3. Roll the apples in antioxidant (optional).
4. Slice the apples into rings, ¼ inch thick.
5. Dip each slice into an antioxidant (optional). Blot off the extra liquid.
6. Measure and record in Table 2 the total of the diameters.
7. Measure and record in Table 2 the total weight of the rings.
8. Spread the apple rings on a wooden rack (or on a thin board that has been covered with layers of paper towels).
9. Place the rack and apples in the center of the oven.
10. Leave the oven door open a crack to let the water vapor escape. Keep the temperature at 150°F.
11. Turn the apples every half hour until they are rubbery and tough (4 or 5 hours). If necessary, turn off the oven overnight and start the next day.
12. Measure and record in Table 2 the total of the diameters. Figure the loss in size.
13. Measure and record in Table 2 the total weight of the rings. Figure the loss in weight.
14. Figure how much of the apples was water.

Table 2.   Size and Weight Loss in Dried Apples

NUMBER OF APPLE RINGS N = _____	TOTAL OF THE DIAMETERS OF APPLE RINGS	WEIGHT OF APPLE RINGS AND PIE PAN	−	WEIGHT OF PIE PAN	=	NET WEIGHT OF APPLE RINGS
Before drying	A _____	_____	−	_____	=	D _____
After drying	B _____	_____	−	_____	=	E _____
Total loss in diameter (A–B = C)	A _____ − B _____ = C _____		Weight of water lost (D–E)			D _____ −E _____ = _____
Average loss in diameter (C ÷ N)	C _____ ÷ N _____ = _____					

Absorption Experiment:
Cooking Dried Lima Beans

Ingredients

¾ cup dried lima beans
3 cups water
1 small carrot, chopped
1 small onion, chopped
½ teaspoon dried basil, or
2 teaspoons chopped fresh basil
¾ teaspoon salt
butter (optional)

Directions

1. Set aside 3 or 4 dried beans for step 4 and weigh the rest. Record the weight in Table 3.
2. Put the beans and water into a saucepan. Bring to a boil.
3. Remove from heat and cover tightly. Let sit for at least 2 hours.
4. Remove the beans from the liquid with a slotted spoon. Weigh them and record their weight in Table 3. Figure the weight of the water absorbed by the beans. Compare the size and weight of these beans with the size and weight of the dried beans.
5. Return the beans to the liquid in the saucepan. Bring them to a boil. Simmer for 40 minutes, checking periodically. Add more water, if necessary, to keep beans from sticking to the pan.
6. Add carrots, onions, basil, and salt when the beans are soft.
7. Cover and simmer for 8 minutes.
8. Use a slotted spoon to drain off the broth. Serve.
9. Put a slice of butter on top of each serving (optional).

Table 3. Weight Gain from Cooking Dried Beans

	WEIGHT OF BEANS AND PIE PAN	−	WEIGHT OF PIE PAN	=	NET WEIGHT OF BEANS
Before cooking and soaking	_____	−	_____	=	A _____
After cooking and soaking	_____	−	_____	=	B _____
			Weight of water absorbed (B−A)		B _____ −A _____ = _____
			How many times heavier are the cooked beans than the dried beans?		B _____ ÷A _____ = _____

Coagulation Experiment:
Preparing Hard-Boiled Eggs

Ingredients

4 eggs
water

Directions

1. Fill a saucepan half full of water.
2. Bring the water to a boil.
3. While the water heats, puncture an end of each egg with a pin.
4. Lower the eggs into the boiling water with a slotted spoon.
5. Boil the eggs over low heat for 15 minutes. Do not let the water boil away. Add more, if needed.
6. Lift each egg from the saucepan with a slotted spoon.
7. Plunge it at once into a bowl of cold water. This will keep the shell from sticking to the egg white.
8. When the eggs are cool, crack one to see if it has become coagulated.
9. Refrigerate the other eggs for later use in "Making Deviled Eggs."

Coagulation Experiment:
Making Deviled Eggs

Ingredients

3 hard-boiled eggs
2 teaspoons lemon juice
1 teaspoon mayonnaise
⅛ teaspoon dry mustard
⅛ teaspoon salt
dash of black pepper
paprika

Directions

1. Remove the shells from the eggs.
2. Cut each egg in half lengthwise.
3. Remove the yolks. Put them into a shallow dish.
4. Mash the yolks with a fork.
5. Add the lemon juice, mayonnaise, dry mustard, salt, and pepper.
6. Mash again until the mixture is smooth.
7. Spread the mixture evenly on the bottom of the dish. Divide it into six equal parts.
8. With a spoon, put ⅙ of the mixture into each egg white half.
9. Sprinkle the filled eggs with paprika.

Coagulation Experiment:
Making a Cheese Omelet

Ingredients

4 eggs
¼ teaspoon salt
2 tablespoons salad oil
1 tablespoon grated Parmesan cheese

Directions

1. Measure the ingredients. Put them near the stove.
2. Break the eggs into a bowl.
3. Heat the frying pan over medium heat.
4. Put a serving plate near the stove.
5. Whisk the eggs with a fork just enough to blend them.
6. Check the pan to see if it is hot enough. Do this by sprinkling a few drops of water into the pan. The drops should dance in the pan, if it is hot enough.

7. When the pan is hot enough, pour in the salad oil. Spread it around with a spatula.
8. Sprinkle the salt over the surface of the pan.
9. Pour the egg mixture into the pan.
10. Count 10 seconds.
11. Sprinkle the grated cheese on the eggs.
12. Let the omelet become a little bit firm. Fold it in half with two forks or a spatula.
13. Cook the omelet for another minute.
14. Slide the omelet from the pan onto the serving plate.
15. Use a spatula to divide the omelet and serve it.

Softening Experiment:
Making a Cooked Vegetable Platter

Ingredients

1 medium carrot

2 stalks celery, or
4 asparagus stalks

6 brussels sprouts, or
¼ head cabbage

¼ head cauliflower, or
¼ head broccoli

1 zucchini squash, or
1 yellow summer squash

2 ears corn, or
2 dozen pea pods

butter, salt, and pepper for seasoning

Directions

1. Wash and prepare the vegetables as follows: Slice carrot, celery, asparagus, cabbage, and squash. Cut brussels sprouts in half from end to end. Break or cut cauliflower (or broccoli) at the small stems. Cut corn from the cob (or hull peas).
2. Set aside a small portion of each vegetable to eat raw.
3. Bring 1 inch of water to boil in the saucepan.
4. Place each group of vegetables on a steam rack over the water. Or, gently lower them into the water.
5. Cover the saucepan. Steam or boil the vegetables 5–10 minutes, just until tender.
6. Serve a portion of each vegetable to each person.
7. Add butter, salt, and pepper to season.
8. Compare the cooked and raw portions of each vegetable.

Softening Experiment:
Making Twice-Baked Potatoes

Ingredients

3 medium potatoes
½ teaspoon salt
3 tablespoons butter (use guide marks on
    wrapper to measure)
3 tablespoons of milk if using Idaho
    potatoes

Directions

1. Bake potatoes ¾–1 hour in a 400°F. oven.
2. Cut the potatoes in half lengthwise.
3. Scoop the pulp from the potato skins with a small spoon.
4. Mash the pulp with salt and butter, and milk if using it.
5. Fill the skins with the mashed potatoes. Squeeze it through a pastry bag to make a pretty pattern (optional).
6. Bake the filled skins in a shallow pan for 15 minutes at 400°F. or until the tops are golden brown.

Thickening Experiment:
Making Popcorn

Ingredients

⅓ cup popcorn kernels
2 tablespoons salad oil
salt

Directions

1. Place 3 popcorn kernels and salad oil in a saucepan.
2. Cover the pan and heat it quickly.
3. When 2 or 3 kernels have popped, add the remaining kernels.
4. Cover and agitate the pan. Do this without stopping, over medium-high heat.
5. Listen for the corn to start and then stop popping.
6. Remove the pan from the heat. Cool the popcorn slightly.
7. Sprinkle the popcorn with salt.

Thickening Experiment:
Making Polenta

Ingredients

½ cup cornmeal

1½ cups water

½ teaspoon salt

¼ pound cheddar cheese, grated

Directions

1. Put cornmeal and salt into the top part of a double boiler.
2. Stir water into the cornmeal.
3. Place the pot over water that is boiling in the bottom part of the double boiler.
4. Stir without stopping until the cornmeal thickens (about 5 minutes).
5. Cover and let the cornmeal cook for 20 minutes.
6. Grate the cheese while the cornmeal is cooking.
7. When the cornmeal is cooked, stir in the cheese until it melts.
8. Serve immediately. Or, cool, slice, and fry until brown in a little oil.

Thickening Experiment:
Making Creamed Celery

Ingredients

4 stalks celery with leaves
2 tablespoons butter
2 tablespoons flour
1 cup milk
¼ cup shelled almonds
¼ teaspoon salt

Directions

1. Melt the butter over low heat in another saucepan.
2. Stir in the flour.
3. Add the milk slowly while whisking the mixture.
4. Whisk the sauce until it thickens, then remove from heat.
5. Wash the celery. Cut the stalks into slices ⅜ inch thick. Measure a sample with a ruler.
6. Chop the celery leaves.
7. Steam the celery stalks and leaves on a steaming rack over boiling water for 10–15 minutes. Or, boil in ½ cup water. Cook until just tender.
8. Chop the almonds while the celery cooks.
9. Add the celery, nuts, and salt to the sauce and return mixture to heat.
10. Stir while heating.
11. Serve.

Separation Experiment:
Making Mayonnaise

Ingredients

(Keep them as cold as possible.)
2 egg yolks
1 tablespoon vinegar
1 tablespoon lemon juice
½ teaspoon salt
1 cup salad oil
carrot and celery sticks (optional)

Directions

1. Separate the egg yolk from the egg white as follows: Carefully crack the egg in half over a bowl. Pass the yolk back and forth from one shell half to the other until all the white has dropped into the bowl.

2. Place the yolks in a deep mixing bowl.

3. Freeze or refrigerate the whites to use in making meringue.

4. Squeeze a lemon. Measure the juice.

5. Add lemon juice, vinegar, and salt to the egg yolks.

6. Beat these ingredients with an egg-beater until they are blended.

7. Measure the salad oil.

8. One person should continue beating the ingredients while another person adds oil. Add the oil ¼ teaspoon at a time, until all the oil is emulsified.

9. Serve the mayonnaise with celery and carrot sticks (optional). Or, use it in making deviled eggs. Keep leftover mayonnaise in the refrigerator.

Table 4. Effects of Beating on Different Food Substances

WHAT SUBSTANCES?	WHAT HAPPENS?	WHAT IS CHANGED?	WHAT IS THE PRODUCT?
oil and egg yolk	oil separated in small droplets; droplets coated with egg yolk, which keeps them from coalescing	oil spread through egg	mayonnaise
protein molecules of egg white	molecules stretched out and separated from each other	protein strands form a network to trap air	meringue
drops of butterfat in cream	milk coating beaten off, and separated from, drops of fat	fat droplets coalesce, flow into each other, and make a network to trap air and liquid	whipped cream
		continued beating forces air and liquid out, leaving solid mass	butter

Separation Experiment:
Making Meringue Shells

Ingredients

⅓ cup egg whites (about 3 large eggs) at
    room temperature
¼ teaspoon cream of tartar
¼ teaspoon salt
¾ cup sifted sugar

Directions

1. Turn on the oven to 200°F.
2. Cover a cookie sheet with brown paper. Oil the paper with butter.
3. Add cream of tartar and salt to the egg whites in a mixing bowl.
4. Beat the egg whites with an eggbeater until stiff but not dry.
5. Add sugar, one teaspoon at a time. One person should continue beating while another person sprinkles the sugar over the egg whites.
6. Keep beating until the mixture doesn't sound gritty in the bowl.
7. Make six small piles of meringue on the oiled paper. Shape them with a spoon into little bowls. Swirl the edges with the back of the spoon for a pretty effect.
8. Bake the meringue shells for one hour or until they sound crisp when lightly tapped.
9. Let them cool in a closed oven for a few hours, or they will crack from sudden temperature change.
10. Remove the shells from the paper with a spatula. Store them in a closed container. Refrigerate or freeze them until you are ready to serve them with fruit and whipped cream.

Separation Experiment:
Making Whipped Cream

Ingredients

½ pint (1 cup) whipping cream
1 teaspoon vanilla

Directions

1. Beat the cream in a bowl until it stands in peaks when you lift out the egg-beater. Be careful to stop at this point, or you will turn the whipped cream into butter. Keeping the bowl and cream cold will help prevent butter from forming.
2. Add the vanilla. Beat in gently.

3. Serve the whipped cream on top of fresh fruit or fruit-filled meringue shells.

Leavening Experiment:
Making Apple Puffs

Ingredients

1 egg
1 tablespoon sugar
¼ teaspoon cinnamon
¼ teaspoon nutmeg
1 cup tart apples, grated (about 3 medium apples)
⅜ cup sifted all-purpose flour
2 egg whites
dash of salt

Directions

1. Beat a whole egg in a bowl.
2. Add the sugar, cinnamon, and nutmeg.
3. Peel and grate the apples.
4. Blend the apples and the flour into the egg mixture.
5. Beat the egg whites and salt with an eggbeater in another bowl.
6. Fold the egg whites into the apple mixture gently.
7. Heat and oil the griddle.
8. Drop the batter by tablespoons onto the griddle. The puffs should expand to about 2 inches in diameter.
9. Lift the puffs with a spatula to check when their bottoms have turned golden brown.
10. Turn. Cook the other side. Serve at once.

Leavening Experiment:
Watching Yeast and Baking Soda in Action

Ingredients

2 tablespoons honey
2 tablespoons vinegar
3 tablespoons baking soda
3 tablespoons yeast

YEAST IN ACTION

Directions

1. Measure 3 cups of warm water. Use a thermometer to make sure the water is 90–100°F.
2. Pour 1 cup of warm water into each of 3 glasses.
3. Add 1 tablespoon yeast to each glass.
4. Label the glasses "honey," "vinegar," and "control."
5. Add the following to the right glasses:
   a. one tablespoon honey
   b. one tablespoon vinegar
   c. nothing ("control")

6. Keep the glasses warm. Place them near a heat source or in a pan of warm water. Every 2 minutes, watch and listen to the results.

BAKING SODA IN ACTION

Directions

1. Measure 3 cups of warm water. Use a thermometer to make sure the water is 90–100°F.
2. Pour 1 cup of warm water into each of 3 glasses.
3. Add 1 tablespoon baking soda to each glass.
4. Label the glasses "honey," "vinegar," and "control."
5. Watch and listen to the results as you add the following to the right glasses:
   a. one tablespoon honey
   b. one tablespoon vinegar
   c. nothing ("control")

Leavening Experiment:
Growing Wheat Sprouts

Ingredients

½ cup wheat grains
warm water

Directions

1. Place wheat grains in a quart jar.
2. Cover the jar top with mesh.
3. Use rubber bands around the jar top to hold the mesh in place.
4. Pour a cup of warm water through the mesh.
5. Let the grains soak for a few hours in a dark place.
6. Pour off the water through the mesh.
7. Pour more warm water into the jar. Pour it off. Rinse the grain this way several times.
8. Invert the jar to drain off the water.
9. Set the jar in a dark place so that germination of the grains can take place.
10. Repeat steps 7, 8, and 9 twice a day until the grains have sprouted about ½ inch.
11. Invert the jar. Set it at an angle in a light place for a day. The leaf buds will turn slightly green.
12. Taste the sprouts. Or, sprinkle them on top of a vegetable salad or put them in a sandwich.

Leavening Experiment:
Making Wheat Germ Pancakes with Baking Powder

Ingredients

Divide the ingredients in half to serve 6 people:

____ 1 cup whole wheat flour

____ ½ cup wheat germ

____ ½ cup powdered milk

____ 1 teaspoon salt

____ 2 teaspoons baking powder

____ 1½ cups water

____ 1 tablespoon honey

____ 2 eggs

____ 2 tablespoons vegetable oil

butter (optional)

Directions

1. Measure the dry ingredients into a large bowl. Blend.
2. Beat the liquid ingredients together in a small bowl with an eggbeater.
3. Make a hole in the center of the dry ingredients.
4. Pour the liquid ingredients into the hole.
5. Stir the mixture until all the ingredients are blended. Stir one minute longer to make the gluten elastic.
6. Place a griddle over medium heat.
7. Sprinkle a few water drops on the griddle to test for heat. When water drops dance on the griddle, grease it with oil using a spatula.
8. Drop the batter by spoonfuls onto the griddle.
9. Turn the pancakes when bubbles appear. Brown the pancakes on both sides.
10. Serve the pancakes at once. Top with butter (optional).

Leavening Experiment:
Making Wheat Germ Pancakes with Yeast

Ingredients

Divide the ingredients in half to serve 6 people:

____ 1 cup whole wheat flour

____ ½ cup wheat germ

____ ½ cup powdered milk

____ 1 teaspoon salt

____ 2 tablespoons baker's yeast

____ 1½ cups warm water (90°F)

____ 1 tablespoon honey

____ 2 eggs

____ 2 tablespoons vegetable oil

butter (optional)

Directions

1. Pour the warm water into a large bowl. Stir in the yeast and honey.
2. Measure the dry ingredients into a small bowl.
3. Add the eggs and oil to the liquid mixture. Beat with an eggbeater.
4. Add the dry ingredients to the liquid ingredients.
5. Stir the mixture until all of the ingredients are blended. Stir one minute longer to make the gluten elastic.
6. Place a griddle over medium heat.
7. Sprinkle a few water drops on the griddle to test for heat. When water drops dance on the griddle, grease it with oil using a spatula.
8. Drop the batter by spoonfuls onto the griddle.
9. Turn the pancakes when bubbles appear. Brown the pancakes on both sides.
10. Serve the pancakes at once. Top with butter (optional).

Sensory Perception Experiment:
Identifying Herbs

Ingredients

A selection of both fresh and dried herbs,
    taken from the following:

basil
chives
mint
oregano
parsley
rosemary
sage
thyme

Directions

1. Crush and smell some of the leaves of
   each herb plant.

2. Look at the shapes and textures of the
   leaves of each plant. How are they the
   same? Different?

3. On the chart or on drawing paper,
   draw a leaf from each plant, exactly as
   you see it. Smell the herb while you
   draw.

4. Work in pairs. One person should
   close his or her eyes while the other
   person holds some crushed herb
   leaves near the partner's nose. See if
   the partner can identify the herb by
   smell. Then, switch places.

5. Smell the leaves of the dried herbs.
   Compare the fresh and dried leaves of
   the same herb. How are they the same?
   Different?

Herb Leaves

basil	chives	mint	oregano
parsley	rosemary	sage	thyme

Sensory Perception Experiment:
Making Cheese Tom Ditty

Ingredients

6 slices bread

1 can (10½ ounces) condensed tomato
    soup

1 cup cheddar cheese, grated

¼ teaspoon dried oregano

Directions

1. Toast the bread in a 350°F. oven (or
   toaster) until golden brown or crisp.
   One person should check the bread in
   the oven every minute.
2. Grate the cheese.
3. Heat the condensed tomato soup in a
   saucepan over medium heat until it
   begins to bubble. Whisk it constantly.
4. One person should continue whisking
   while another person slowly adds the
   cheese. When the cheese is melted,
   take the pan from the heat.
5. Rub the dried oregano in the palm of
   your hand until it is crushed. Add it to
   the cheese and tomato mixture.
6. Place the toast on individual plates.
   Cut each slice into four triangles.
7. Spoon the cheese and tomato mixture
   over the toast triangles on each plate.

Sensory Perception Experiment: Making Celery Logs with Chives

Ingredients

3 ounces cream cheese
10–15 chive leaves
3 large, or 6 small, stalks celery

Directions

1. Set out the cream cheese in a small bowl to soften at room temperature.
2. Wash celery stalks. Cut them into 2 inch lengths. Measure a sample with a ruler.
3. Chop the chives by snipping them with scissors. They should be ⅛ inch or less in length.
4. Use a fork to blend the chives with the cream cheese.
5. Spread the mixture into the groove of each celery section, using a small knife.

Sensory Perception Experiment:
Making Spiced Cabbage

Ingredients

2 cups green cabbage, grated
1 cup purple cabbage, grated
½ cup water
2 tablespoons vinegar
5 whole cloves
½ teaspoon allspice
⅛ teaspoon pepper
1 tablespoon brown sugar
¼ teaspoon salt
1½ tablespoons butter

Directions

1. Grate the cabbage.
2. Put the water, vinegar, cloves, allspice, pepper, and brown sugar into a skillet.
3. Cover the skillet. Bring the liquid to a boil over medium heat.
4. Add the cabbage. Heat and stir it.
5. Cover the skillet. Turn the heat to low.
6. Simmer for 12–15 minutes, or until the cabbage is softened.
7. Remove the cloves. Add the salt.
8. Stir the butter into the cabbage until it melts. Serve.